ng about

Capitalism vs. Freedom

The ravages of the neoliberal assault on the global population have by now reached the point where they are literally threatening decent survival, not in the distant future. This eloquent study reveals clearly the roots of the problems and their severe dimensions, and calls for renewal of the inspiring vision of libertarian socialism that was displaced and marginalized through the past century but can be revived within the guidelines that are outlined here, expanding on important initiatives already underway.

Noam Chomsky

In many ways the consciousness and propensities of young people in the US give reason to be optimistic about the future. On average our young generation is less racist, less homophobic, less sexist, and less militaristic than its forbears. In addition to these admirable characteristics, young Americans are also freedom loving, which is where Larson's book comes in. In the US more than anywhere else the cause of "freedom" has been appropriated by right-wing libertarians as a powerful ideological vehicle to gain political support for a conservative political agenda—to the point where if you tell a young American that you are a "libertarian socialist" they look at you in utter confusion, as if you have contradicted yourself in only two words. With a welcome sense of humor, Larson focuses on examining what freedom means and does not mean, why the right-wing libertarian political agenda subverts freedom rather than promotes it, and why a libertarian socialist program is how young Americans can achieve the freedom they long for.

Robin Hahnel

Capitalism
vs.
Freedom

Capitalism vs. Freedom

Rob Larson

Winchester, UK
Washington, USA

First published by Zero Books, 2018
Zero Books is an imprint of John Hunt Publishing Ltd., No. 3 East Street,
Alresford, Hampshire SO24 9EE, UK
office1@jhpbooks.net
www.johnhuntpublishing.com
www.zero-books.net

For distributor details and how to order please visit the 'Ordering' section on our website.

ISBN: 978 1 78535 733 6
978 1 78535 734 3 (ebook)
Library of Congress Control Number: 2017940002

A CIP catalogue record for this book is available from the British Library.

Design: Stuart Davies

Printed and bound by CPI Group (UK) Ltd, Croydon, CR0 4YY, UK

We operate a distinctive and ethical publishing philosophy in all areas of our business, from our global network of authors to production and worldwide distribution.

Contents

We have been cursed with the reign of gold long enough.

Eugene Debs, *Chicago Railway Times*, 1 January 1897

Introduction

What is Freedom?

This is a book about freedom. Before looking into how our economic system helps or hurts human freedom, it's worth thinking about what freedom is. Most of us think of freedom as what you do when nothing's stopping you. It's the ability to do what you want, within the limits of your free time and budget. That's a good start, because it reminds us why we care about freedom in the first place. Because whatever you like to do, whoever you love, whatever makes you laugh or feel fulfilled, those things represent the value of social freedom to you. Whatever way you to like to waste your time, whichever career option you're free to follow or regret following, represent the fruits of freedom. How much freedom you have decides how much fun, adventure, enrichment, growth, peace and love you get to enjoy in your limited human years.

John Stuart Mill's "On Liberty" is considered to be one of the founding philosophical essays on freedom, and it takes the position that freedom is about "the nature and limits of the power which can be legitimately exercised by society over the individual."[1] Mill's view was that "in things which do not primarily concern others, individuality should assert itself," and "the sole end for which mankind are warranted, individually or collectively in interfering with the liberty of action of any of their number, is self-protection... the only purpose for which power can be rightfully exercised over any member of a civilized community, against his will, is to prevent harm to others."[2]

So the concept of *power* appears quickly in any discussion of freedom. Social power means the ability to direct the actions of other people, to make an individual or group do what you want. Power may be exercised in different forms by different groups

1

or institutions, but since it means forcing people to do things against their will, it's considered to be antagonistic to liberty and freedom. For this reason, reductions of the power held within a society are thought to expand freedom—for example, if a government loses its power to police what people say, freedom of speech is therefore expanded. Often, related freedoms are grouped together and referred to as "rights" that individuals should possess, like the right to a free speech.

Mill wasn't absolute in these principles, concluding that "There are also many positive acts for the benefit of others, which [a person] may rightfully be compelled to perform; such as, to give evidence in a court of justice; to bear his fair share in the common defence, or in any other joint work necessary to the interest of the society of which he enjoys the protection..."[3] But, since the use of power or compulsion means forcing people to do things they wouldn't do otherwise, it's considered to be antagonistic to personal liberty and the burden of justification is on the supporter of using force.

So Mill's basic view was that power had to be limited, in order to protect a realm of freedom of action for individuals. This basic picture, in which freedom is mainly seen to be an absence of power and coercion over people, was described as "negative freedom" by the Russian-British philosopher Isaiah Berlin in his influential essay "Two Concepts of Liberty." Berlin outlined a pair of complementary concepts of freedom, with negative liberty being essentially what Mill supported, "that there ought to exist a certain minimum area of personal freedom which must on no account be violated," and recognizing that "Where it is to be drawn is a matter of argument, indeed of haggling."[4] But he also observed that negative liberty has limits, since "liberty in this sense is not incompatible with some kinds of autocracy," where "a liberal-minded despot would allow his subjects a large measure of personal freedom. The despot who leaves his subjects a wide area of liberty may be unjust, or encourage the wildest inequalities, care little for order, for virtue, or knowledge; but provided he does not curb their liberty, or at least curbs it less than many other regimes, he meets with Mill's specification [of negative freedom]. Freedom in this sense is not, at any rate logically, connected with democracy or self-government."[5]

Recognizing this, Berlin also described "positive liberty," which asks what we are free to actually do, rather than how much we're constrained by power. Instead of asking, "How much do society's power centers limit my freedom?" positive freedom asks, "What am I free to do?" or "What power centers decide what I'm free to do?" The difference is sometimes represented as the ideal of negative freedom, or "freedom from," where liberty is unconstrained by some external power, on the one hand; and on the other, the positive liberty of "freedom to" do different things, like the right to share in an economy's prosperity, or the right to vote and have a say in how collective decisions get made.

Positive freedoms people might have could evolve over time, with the society's material standard of living. It wouldn't make much sense to say a medieval farmer was being oppressed because he or she wasn't free to become a cosmetic surgeon—the society's level of wealth and knowledge at that time didn't allow many people to do much beside produce food. Once a society develops to the point that people are free to specialize and develop sophisticated skills, we might say that a young person should be free, or have a right, to study to become a surgeon if they choose.

Amartya Sen, the Nobel Prize-winning Indian economist, made this point when he wrote that "Sometimes the lack of substantive freedoms relates directly to economic poverty, which robs people of the freedom to satisfy hunger, or to achieve sufficient nutrition, or to obtain remedies for treatable illnesses, or the opportunity to be adequately clothed or sheltered, or to enjoy clean water or sanitary facilities."[6] Sen's point was that to the extent that an economy can afford these services for the population, their lack of a positive "freedom to" use and benefit from them is a real limit to liberty, a situation often seen in "the persistence of deprivations among segments of the community that happen to remain excluded" from society's wealth.[7]

On the other hand, Berlin was skeptical of overreach in the scope of positive freedom, suggesting it could be exploited by authoritarians to control individual behavior, on the grounds they should be free to order people around to achieve their ambitions. This would make positive liberty "at times, no better than a specious disguise for brutal tyranny."[8] However, Berlin was quite clear that there was value to both categories of freedom, saying "the satisfaction that each of them seeks is an ultimate value which... has an equal right to be classed among the deepest interests of mankind." And he suggested "Perhaps the chief value for liberals of political—'positive'—rights, of participating in the government, is as a means for protecting what they hold to be an ultimate value, namely individual—'negative'—liberty."[9] So the positive freedom to decide, with your fellow citizens, the policies of social power centers like governments, itself helps protect your personal negative freedom. And indeed, a careful reading of Mill's own classic essay indicates that he realized "men might as well be imprisoned, as excluded from the means of earning their bread."[10] Even in a work mainly focused on negative freedom, Mill recognized the value of positive freedom.

Many other figures have debated the subject, with different conclusions that cut across political lines. The conservative economist Frank Knight of the University of Chicago wrote that opponents of the positive view of freedom "overlook that fact that freedom to perform an act is meaningless unless the subject is in possession of the requisite means of action."[11] This is a classic argument for positive freedom, the freedom *to* pursue various actions, although Knight himself was skeptical of the distinction. On the other side of the political spectrum, the Marxist philosopher Erich Fromm also held that freedom from powerful people or institutions wasn't enough, and that people might in fact "try to escape from freedom altogether unless they can progress from negative to positive freedom."[12]

On the other hand, the arch-libertarian economic Murray Rothbard wrote that to his mind, the word "free" meant simply "being unmolested by other persons."[13] Similarly, the prominent eighteenth-century Prussian philosopher Wilhelm von Humboldt strongly opposed positive freedom, even including "all measures employed to remedy or prevent natural devastations," which even supporters of only negative freedom alone are usually prepared to accept.[14]

But despite this philosophical debate about the complexities of the nature of freedom, the thinkers who actively shaped today's economic policies took a relatively simple view of the issue. In his 1962 book *Capitalism and Freedom*, economist Milton Friedman wrote that "The fundamental threat to freedom is power to coerce, be it in the hands of a monarch, a dictator, an oligarchy, or a momentary majority. The preservation of freedom requires the elimination of such concentration of power to the fullest possible extent and the dispersal and distribution of whatever power cannot be eliminated—a system of checks and balances."[15] So Friedman stands closer to Humboldt and partially Berlin, saying that limiting power will increase the negative freedom of individuals, spreading their scope of independent action.

Friedrich Hayek agreed, writing in his prominent book *The Road to Serfdom* that "'Freedom' and 'liberty' are now words so worn with use and abuse that one must hesitate to employ them to express the ideals for which they stood." Like Friedman, Hayek favored a concept of liberty keeping fairly strictly to the negative version of freedom from external constraint, describing how "During the whole of this modern period of European history the general direction of social development was one of freeing the individual from the ties which had bound him to the customary or prescribed ways in the pursuit of his ordinary activities."[16]

Friedman's *Capitalism and Freedom* and Hayek's *The Road to Serfdom* promoted the argument that free-market capitalism was the social arrangement that most encouraged human freedom. The books' arguments gained more prominence in the decades that followed and in the 1980s these views became the basis for a good deal of government policy, from the Reagan administration and Thatcher government in the US and UK, to Deng Xiaoping and Augusto Pinochet in China and Chile.

The debate among these views is usually described as breaking roughly along political lines—conservatives and libertarians take the view that negative freedom is best, citing reservations like Berlin's, and that this freedom is provided by markets. More liberal commenters accept negative freedom, but also think some form of positive freedom is required (usually from the public sector), as in Sen's and Knight's arguments above. The schools broadly agree that capitalism provides negative liberty.

This book makes the argument that capitalism and markets fail the tests for *both* categories of freedom. Capitalism withholds opportunities to enjoy freedom (required by the positive view of freedom) and also encourages the growth of economic power (the adversary of liberty in the negative view of freedom). The book's focus will be on power within capitalism, and therefore on the negative picture of freedom, since this is considered to be promoted by market economics, and because it's the part of the definition of freedom on which people most broadly agree. However, the important positive concept of liberty will also appear often.

This argument begins in Chapter 1, which looks at the different forms of economic power that are created in markets, as wealth and market shares become concentrated in fewer and fewer hands. Chapter 2 extends this market analysis to the media and information networks, owing to their special importance in providing the means for individual freedom of thought and social action. Chapter 3 reviews the frequently decisive control that concentrated wealth has over government policy, Chapter 4 projects modern environmental trends to map the freedom of future generations, and Chapter 5 turns from capitalism to other economic systems that might both constrain economic power and provide more positive freedom, as well.

So this is a book about freedom and therefore a book about power. Consider yourself free to read.

Endnotes

1. John Stuart Mill, *On Liberty*, Mineola, NY: Dover, 2002, p. 1.
2. *Ibid*, p. 47, 8.
3. *Ibid*, p. 9.
4. Isaiah Berlin, *Four Essays On Liberty*, New York: Oxford University Press, 1969, p. 124.
5. *Ibid*, p. 129–30.
6. Amartya Sen, *Development As Freedom*, New York: Anchor Books, 2000, p. 4.
7. *Ibid*, p. 7.
8. Berlin, *Four Essays On Liberty*, p. 131.
9. *Ibid*, p. 166, 165.
10. Mill, *On Liberty*, p. 26.
11. Frank Knight, *Freedom and Reform*, New York: Harper & Brothers, 1982, p. 7.
12. Erich Fromm, *Escape From Freedom*, New York: Ishi Press, 2011, p. 134.
13. Murray Rothbard, *Man, Economy and State with Power and Market*, Auburn, AL: Ludwig von Mises Institute, 2009, p. 654.
14. Willhelm von Humboldt, *The Limits of State Action*, Indianapolis, IN: Liberty Fund, 1993, p. 17.
15. Milton Friedman, *Capitalism and Freedom*, Chicago, IL:

University of Chicago Press, 2002, p. 15.

16. Friedrich Hayek, *The Road to Serfdom*, Chicago: University of Chicago Press, 2007, p. 68, 69.

Chapter 1

Classes and Crashes
Freedom of Work

Masters are always and everywhere in a sort of tacit, but constant and uniform combination, not to raise the wages of labour... Such combinations, however, are frequently resisted by a contrary defensive combination of the workmen... It is not, however, difficult to foresee which of the two parties must, upon all ordinary occasions, have the advantage in the dispute, and force the others into a compliance with their terms. The masters, being fewer in number, can combine much more easily; and the law, besides, authorizes, or at least does not prohibit their combinations, while it prohibits those of the workmen.
Adam Smith[1]

Experience demonstrates that there may be a slavery of wages only a little less galling and crushing in its effects than chattel slavery, and that this slavery of wages must go down with the other... those who would reproach us should remember that it is hard for labor, however fortunately and favorably surrounded, to cope with the tremendous power of capital in any contest for higher wages or improved condition.
Frederick Douglass[2]

In the twenty-first century a rising wave of men and women globally are seeing alarming failures of our social system, and frustration is growing because many people don't feel free to fix things. Americans told the Gallup opinion polling agency in 2014 that they are less and less happy with their "freedom to choose what you do with your life," with reported satisfaction dropping to 79 percent.[3] A BBC World Service poll also found people's belief that media are free has fallen around the world, with confidence in the UK, US and Germany falling below 50 percent.[4] Less than half of respondents felt free to safely express their opinions online, not only in Russia and China, but also Australia and Mexico. These tumbling numbers are leading people around the world to search for answers about their weakened freedoms.

One heavily promoted road to freedom follows figures like Milton Friedman and Friedrich Hayek, whose ideas are reliably featured on more conservative media like US talk radio and New Corporation properties from the UK to Brazil. Friedman's central claim was that capitalism, or a "free market" system, leaves consumers "free to choose" among different goods and jobs, while Hayek is most associated with a complementary opposition to government policies like income taxes or broader social "planning," which many would now call "big government." Hayek held that these policies were in fact a "Road to Serfdom," because they meant more government power in the economy, threatening to reduce us to the condition of unfree "serfs" — the helpless economic semi-slaves of the feudal economic system that preceded capitalism.

But while this view has continued to be promoted on the most dominant commercial media, there are some problems. The issue reviewed in this chapter is the problem of *power* — whether authority is mainly held by government, as Friedman and Hayek claim, or whether large amounts of money could also mean significant social power. An honest look at these subjects can help us understand a puzzling statement by billionaire Nick Hanauer, a hugely successful investor and a cofounder of Amazon.com. In an article written for "My Fellow Zillionaires," Hanauer disagrees with these prominent economists when they dismiss income inequality — the gap between the incomes at the top of society and the average household. Hanauer credits his business success to his strong foresight, and writes that today he sees "pitchforks" because "inequality is at historically high levels and getting worse every day," warning that the US and the world are turning into "a feudal society."[5]

So which is the real road back to the Dark Ages and a loss of freedom? Is it growth of government functions in society, the regulations and taxation that Hayek claimed would lead to "serfdom?" Or is it the growth of towering fortunes and corporate empires that is reducing us to "a feudal society," as the billionaire Hanauer suggests? Let's cross-examine the case for capitalism and see if the books have been cooked.

Atlas Hugged

One of the greatest advocates for the libertarian view of capitalism was the economist Milton Friedman, Nobel Prize winner and maybe the most respected conservative economist in the US. Friedman was an informal economic adviser to conservative US president Ronald Reagan, who said in an interview with the libertarian magazine *Reason* that "I believe the very heart and soul of conservatism is libertarianism."[6] Reagan himself wrote a warm blurb for Friedman's book *Free to Choose* and recorded an endorsement video for Friedman's TV series based on the book, calling the show "something of rare importance."[7] Friedman's policy views had an enormous impact across political lines and media platforms.

And despite his death in 2006, Friedman has remained prominent in today's conservative media. The right-wing radio icon Rush Limbaugh said on his talk program that "Milton Friedman should be the Bible for young people, or anybody, trying to understand capitalism and free markets."[8] When Friedman died, William F. Buckley, considered the dean of conservative intellectuals until his own death in 2008, wrote an obituary of Friedman in the most respected right-wing magazine in the US, *National Review*. He said:

> The period since 1980 has been the Age of Friedman economically... The Age of Friedman began approximately in 1979–80 when his disciples, Margaret Thatcher and Ronald Reagan, took power... And these two leaders embarked on economic policies, broadly inspired by his theories, that have given their countries a quarter century of fast economic growth interrupted only by two short and shallow recessions in the U.S.[9]

Considering the $12 trillion financial cataclysm and semi-depression that followed later in 2008, this warm praise is the tiniest bit ironic now.

So what is this Age of Friedman? Friedman himself proudly summarized in *The Wall Street Journal* the Reagan administration policies he had helped create, including "slashing taxes" and "attacking government regulations," a trend called "deregulation" which has continued to this day.[10] Based on the Friedmans' ideas becoming a major global policy inspiration, the *Review* said of Friedman and his wife and frequent coauthor, Rose, "These two great champions of freedom should recognize that they have won. The course of history is firmly on their side."[11] So today's main economic policy trends, strongly in the direction of tax reduction and economic deregulation, are parts of this Age of Friedman.

Friedman's basic view was that freedom is promoted by markets, which are social arrangements for the buying and selling of goods and services. To visualize a market, you can picture yourself at a mall, or a farmer's market, or shopping online. This "market freedom" had a huge importance, as Friedman wrote in his influential book *Capitalism and Freedom*:

> Economic arrangements play a dual role in the promotion

of a free society. On the one hand, freedom in economic arrangements is itself a component of freedom broadly understood, so economic freedom is an end in itself. In the second place, economic freedom is also an indispensible means toward the achievement of political freedom... Viewed as a means to the end of political freedom, economic arrangements are important because of their effect on the concentration or dispersion of power. The kind of economic organization that provides economic freedom directly, namely, competitive capitalism, also promotes political freedom because it separates economic power from political power and in this way enables the one to offset the other.[12]

Friedman held that these free markets promote freedom because they allow competition, giving consumers and workers the freedom to decide what they want to buy and from whom, and likewise whom to work for. Writing with his wife in *Free to Choose*, he explained that in a free market "When you enter a store, no one forces you to buy. You are free to do so or go elsewhere. That is the basic difference between the market and a political agency. You are free to choose."[13]

This basic picture of market freedom was a main focus of the other most prominent figure of right-wing economics, Friedrich Hayek. He taught at the highly prestigious London School of Economics and the University of Chicago, and later advised conservative governments including Thatcher in the UK and Augusto Pinochet in Chile. He had a more recent popularity boom after being extensively promoted on the popular right-wing *Glenn Beck Program*.[14]

Hayek held that the provision of economic goods and services by government had none of the freedom of the market, and that Western civilization had gone far beyond an appropriate level with its attempts to moderate the market's cycle of growth and recession, called the "business cycle." Hayek called such programs "socialist" and a betrayal of Europe's history of "freeing the individual from the ties which had bound him to the customary or prescribed ways in the pursuit of his ordinary activities." Since then, "We have progressively abandoned that freedom in economic affairs without which personal and political freedom has never existed in the past."[15]

Like Friedman and the broader "libertarian" tradition, Hayek held that markets bring about the maximum of human freedom and unlock human potential. "Economic liberalism... regards competition as superior not only because it is in most circumstances the most efficient method known but even more because it is the only method by which our activities can be adjusted to each other without coercive or arbitrary intervention of authority."[16] This crucial connection, between a "free market" and competition, is usually taken for granted, as it was in Friedman's arguments above.

Other major economists of this tradition on the Right include Murray Rothbard, less prominent than Hayek and the Friedmans but considered a major figure in libertarian and conservative circles. He concluded that markets allow "free association" and that successful businesspeople possess superior qualities: "A man earns profits... by superior foresight and judgment" and "The greater a man's profit has been, the more praiseworthy his role."[17] Profit, of course, is the money made by a business after its basic costs have been paid. Rothbard's argument was also based on the use of profits to pay for new investments by the company, to buy new equipment or build new productive facilities. These investments increase the amount of production in the economy, and can create new jobs and goods, leading economists to refer to businesspeople as "job creators."

A figure with similar views, but far more popular, is Russian-American author Ayn Rand. Rand has long been a mascot for libertarian politics and her book *Atlas Shrugged* is one of the best-selling books in history. Her work is often read among powerful people, yet her work is a crude, comic book version of this same conservative picture of the market economy. To make the concepts a little more obvious for the reader, Rand's infallible executive protagonists are all described as good-looking, and the antagonist workers and regulators are ugly and poorly dressed.[18] Only slightly less shallow is her capitalist characters' tendency to magically run the firm themselves—they both manage their corporate empires directly and also invent the new scientific products and do the striking commercial art and design the buildings. They are truly portrayed as borderline supermen, only based on their power as big businessmen, not their ethnicity.

Many libertarian figures are less extreme than Rand's near-worship of capitalists, like Friedman who wrote more modestly that "the inequality of income" in "large part reflects initial differences in endowment, both of human capacities and of property."[19] But more than Friedman and even more than Rand, the bar for capitalist worship was set by Ludwig von Mises, who is considered to be the founder of the highly conservative Austrian School of economics, to which Hayek and Rothbard belong. Mises wrote about the "Creative Genius" of wealthy entrepreneurs:

> Far above the millions that come and pass away tower the pioneers, the men whose deeds and ideas cut out new paths for mankind. For the pioneering genius to create is the essence of life... For him there is no leisure, only intermissions of temporary sterility and frustration... The accomplishment... does not gratify him mediately because his fellow men at best are unconcerned about it, more often even greet it with taunts, sneers, and persecution... Creating is for him agony and torment, a ceaseless excruciating struggle against internal and external obstacles; it consumes and crushes him.[20]

While Friedman and Hayek implied business people and the rich have little social control, Mises and Rand celebrated CEO power. In fact, Mises was such a fan of Rand's *Atlas Shrugged* that he delightedly wrote to her about their shared views:

> You have the courage to tell the masses what no politician told them: you are inferior and all the improvements in your conditions which you simply take for granted you owe to the effort of men who are better than you.[21]

Business figures themselves only occasionally make arguments similar to these fascists of capital, like the nineteenth-century corporate lawyer John Hay, who claimed "That you have property is proof of industry and foresight on your part or your father's; that you have nothing is a judgment on your laziness and vices, or on your improvidence. The world is a moral world, which it would not be if virtue and vice received the same reward."[22]

As for critics of these views, Friedman wrote in *Capitalism and Freedom* that "a major source of objection to a free economy is precisely that... It gives people what they want instead of what a particular group thinks they ought to want. Underlying most arguments against the free market is a lack of belief in freedom itself."[23] Writers on the Right don't often bother to actually quote an opponent of their views, instead just insisting that they're literally against freedom and moving on. Indeed, Charles Koch, multi-billionaire oil industrialist and a major funder of Tea Party candidates and libertarian think tanks, wrote that opponents of these views support "big government" and believe "that you are incapable of running your own life."[24]

So the traditional right-wing picture of capitalism celebrates the freedom of a creative class of entrepreneurs whose competition creates new industries, lifting up the rest of us in happy employment. It's a view of freedom that starts at the top of society, a picture where the masses should get out of the way of the creative elites. It's a very traditional view, and widely seen on conservative and commercial media around the world. It's also weak-sauce ideology.

The Fun Percent

The first aspect of capitalism to explore, and to evaluate for its relationship to freedom, is its concentration of wealth. Wealth has many forms, including money wealth, like cash and deposits in bank accounts. But it also includes productive wealth, like ownership of agricultural land or industrial property, often through "shares" of corporate stock, which are pieces of ownership of businesses. This second form of wealth is especially important because it produces more wealth—food or products for sale—and profits from their production. These basic forms of wealth are often called "capital."

The connection between freedom and the concentration of wealth has been debated for some time, and the picture painted by the thinkers on the Right is fairly consistent. In *Free to Choose*, for example, the Friedmans are skeptical of:

… the widespread belief that it is not fair that some children should have a great advantage over others simply because they happen to have wealthy parents. Of course it is not fair. However, unfairness can take many forms. It can take the form of the inheritance of property—bonds and stocks, houses, factories; it can also take the form of the inheritance of talent—musical ability, strength, mathematical genius. The inheritance of property can be interfered with more readily than the inheritance of talent. But from an ethical point of view, is there any difference between the two? Yet many people resent the inheritance of property but not the inheritance of talent.[25]

17

Hayek, too, claimed inequality wasn't a major problem: "The fact that the opportunities open to the poor in a competitive society are much more restricted than those open to the rich does not make it less true that in such a society the poor are much more free than a person commanding much greater material comfort in a different type of society."[26] Similarly, Rothbard wrote "That there is inequality of ability or monetary income on the free market should surprise no one. As we have seen above, men are not 'equal' in their tastes, interests, abilities, or locations. Resources are not distributed 'equally' over the earth."[27]

Surely anyone can see the logic of this argument. Very good doctors and carpenters attract more consumer demand, and the prices they charge can then rise, leading to higher incomes for these more talented, harder-working or smarter professionals. The Friedmans' argument was that since humanity cannot control the initial endowment of talents given to each individual, we should likewise have no expectation of controlling unequal endowments of money. This is apparently intended seriously.

But in portraying this concentration of money in society as a reasonable development, the libertarian tradition completely dismisses the *power* of concentrated money. As reviewed in the Introduction, unrestricted power is usually seen as the enemy of freedom, in the most common "negative" concept of liberty. So the phenomenal concentration of wealth of recent history could represent a problem for freedom — "economic power."

Hayek illustrated this conservative skepticism of any influence arising from wealth in *The Road to Serfdom*, a major theme of which is that when the state gains new authority over the economy (by imposing a new tax or creating a new regulation), it gains serious new power. One might conclude from that view that there is power within the market, perhaps in the enormous concentrated fortunes of the modern era, a power that is transferred to the state when it makes a regulatory move. But Hayek draws the issue intriguingly: "To believe that the power which is thus conferred on the state is merely transferred to it from others is erroneous. It is a power newly created and which in a competitive society nobody possesses. So long as property is divided among many owners, none of them acting independently has exclusive power to determine the income and position of particular people," but of course this is the whole point.[28] If wealth, including property, is *not* divided among "many owners" but instead increasingly concentrated in a thin upper crust, Hayek implicitly allows that problems could arise.

And indeed, the political Right does occasionally show some contradiction on the point, as when Friedman writes in *Capitalism and Freedom* about "the role that inequality plays in providing independent foci of power to offset the centralization of political power."[29] However, this concession of the possibility of power flowing from giant fortunes usually comes up only when it can be put as a counterweight to the power of the state. There are exceptions, like when von Mises asked, "on what else is the power of a businessman founded than on his wealth?"[30] The archconservative grudgingly admitted that some anticapitalist critics are "on comparatively better grounds" for wanting "to prohibit the accumulation of wealth precisely because it gives a man economic power."

But despite some of these conservative arguments, the basic power of money is very real—a large amount of money can buy or build very important things in a market society, creating new companies and industries, building up commercial empires over time, and hiring or firing a workforce. It can largely decide the conditions of any employment it provides. Crucially, great wealth decides what industries will be invested in, which ultimately determines what tomorrow's society will look like. One of the most fundamental realities of our modern global society is that money means power and the modern world situation makes it difficult to take seriously Hayek's insistence that economic power is "newly created" when the government steps in.

There are a few particularly important dimensions of this economic power to look at. One is that money knows no inherent limits — an individual's fortune can potentially grow indefinitely, both in absolute terms and relative to the rest of society. While executive and legislative powers in the government are enormous and vitally important to understand, they often have real limits described in founding documents of the world's governments, often based on a "balance of power." Money knows none of these pesky limitations, and over decades gigantic fortunes with incredible power and influence can arise, giving their owners towering importance in society, despite Hayek's "many owners" daydream. The potential scale of this power is illustrated by Wall Street banking titan JP Morgan's bailout of the frigging US federal government itself in 1894. And then again in 1895.[31] Surely the ability, by one lone man's decision, to rescue the economy from depression again and again constitutes tremendous power.

But particularly, more money means you can buy more *freedom*. With a large fortune, you can afford more accountants to free you from your tax burden, more doctors to free you from preventable disease and more attorneys to free you from the consequences of disobeying the civil laws. This, of course, means that as fortunes grow, and rich individuals or families gain wealth and clout, their freedom may expand at the expense of the freedom of others, a development called "hegemonic freedom." This means that the growth of your freedom came at the expense of someone else — for example, if you get a judge to agree you have the positive right to get drunk and hit people, your freedom to commit random violence is increased, yet the negative freedom of other people not to get punched is decreased. This hegemonic freedom simply becomes what we recognize as power, the ability to change the world according to an individual's or group's wishes, and to make others do your will. Bosses have power and anyone who has had a job knows the fundamental work reality of hierarchy, taking orders from upstairs and passing them downstairs.

So, if colossal fortunes are an important means of gaining power and hegemonic freedom, it's natural to review how concentrated wealth has become. One very prominent and comprehensive review of global wealth was done by Thomas Piketty, whose 2014 book *Capital in the Twenty-First Century* caused quite a stir for a long book on economics and inequality. Piketty compiled an enormous database from tax records in the developed world, especially Europe and North America, to study the evolution of capital ownership. His figures on concentration of overall wealth are very striking. Piketty groups US households into deciles, each of which represents 10 percent of the total population, and centiles, each of which constitutes 1 percent of the country. In the US, Piketty finds "By 2010, the top decile's share of total wealth exceeded 70 percent, and the top centile's share was close to 35 percent."[32] In Western Europe, the picture is slightly less severe but similar, with the wealthiest 1 percent owning nearly 30 percent of national wealth in the UK and 23 percent in Germany. China's richest 1 percent holds over a third of the country's wealth.[33]

At the global level, concentration is almost unbelievable, with the worldwide wealth share of "the top centile about 50 percent, and the top decile somewhere between 80 and 90 percent."[34] On the other hand, "half the population own virtually nothing: the poorest 50 percent invariably own less than 10 percent of national wealth... The inescapable reality is this: wealth is so concentrated that a large segment of society is virtually unaware of its existence, so that some people imagine that it belongs to surreal or mysterious entities."[35]

Crucially, Piketty also found that among the wealthiest 1 percent of US households, "shares of stock or partnerships constitute nearly the totality of the largest fortunes... Housing is the favorite investment of the middle class and moderately well-to-do, but true wealth always consists primarily of financial and business assets."[36] This agrees with the work of the Economic Policy Institute, which breaks down the figures on stock ownership: The richest 5 percent of US households in 2010 owned a formidable 67.1 percent of all stock, and the wealthiest 1 percent of households had a staggering 35 percent of traded stock all to itself.[37] Meanwhile, the lower 80 percent of US households held only 8.3 percent of US stock and a large part of that is held passively in retirement accounts.

The scale of wealth concentration has been backed up by Wall Street itself, for example in Citigroup's leaked "plutonomy" memos, describing a condition in which "economic growth is powered by and largely consumed by the wealthy few." Despite the red-faced objections to Occupy Wall Street by many conservatives and libertarians, Citi's own analysts conclude "Clearly, the analysis of the top 1% of US households is paramount."[38] They have also stated they are "generally comfortable with the thrust" of Piketty's own analysis.[39] Other corporate observers have quietly reached similar conclusions, with companies catering to wealthy consumers thriving, while mid-scale firms decline.[40] These widely different approaches arrive at the same conclusion: from nation to nation, there is a small class of phenomenally rich households that do indeed "own the country."

What all this information about wealth concentration means is a *class structure*. Social class refers to the different levels of prestige, wealth and power within a society, whether official or unofficial. Americans are often discouraged from thinking in terms of class, but as labor researcher Katie Quan put it, "not to think in terms of class is unfortunate, since no matter what our ideological persuasion may be, class analysis gives us a way of viewing the world that identifies power relationships. It clarifies who has power,"[41] and indeed class analysis is regularly used in describing *other* societies, whether medieval feudalism or today's Third World dictatorships. In the market economy, four basic classes are discernible, although of course there are many different ways of chopping them up, and I offer these as some basic guidance for conceptualizing the class system.

At the top are the owners of society, the wealthiest few percent who hold those cartoonishly disproportionate shares of capital and overall wealth. This social layer is sometimes called "the ruling class," or more descriptively "the owning class." They are defined not so much by their huge incomes, but by the *source* of that income—primarily the dividends and other revenues from ownership of the productive economy.

At the bottom, of course, are the poor, these days increasingly likely to be unemployed but still composed mostly of the "working poor," those who work part- or full-time yet remain well below an adequate standard of living. They represent something like a fifth of society in developed countries; although there is wide variation and in the global South or "Third World" they make up an enormously larger proportion. They live entirely on their labor incomes and indeed often prematurely die on them.

In between these two classes lies what is often vaguely described as the "middle class;" although a little more precision is helpful. Within this middle realm we can distinguish two similar but distinct classes. One is the "working class," representing the large part of the population in the developed nations that earns a sometimes-decent living, but almost entirely from labor income. This class is associated with "blue collar" jobs, corresponding to the construction workforce, industrial workers, truck drivers, sanitation workers, nurses, teachers and others employed in essential but often low-paid, physically demanding and typically unglamorous work.

The upper part of the middle class can be described as the "professional class," also making their living mostly from work income. This echelon of the social system includes the "white collar" workforce, often doing intellectual work and holding various college or graduate degrees; your doctors, lawyers, engineers, accountants, professors and corporate managers. This class owes the large majority of its income to its education and relatively scarce advanced skills, rather than simple ownership of a large fortune. Families in this class can earn decent amounts up to quite large incomes and sometimes imagine that they are "the rich" or "successful" in society; though they are mostly well below the top levels.

This modern class structure, in the US and around the world, is commonly informal and unspoken, especially in settler countries like the US or Australia with little history of aristocratic deference to remember. Today, few people are born in the US, Europe or China with a definite guarantee to remain in the class of their parents; although in practice this is common. Barbara Ehrenreich pointed out the resulting anxiety of the professional class in her book *Fear of Falling*:

> ... the professional middle class is still only a *middle* class, located well below the ultimate elite of wealth and power. Its only 'capital' is knowledge and skill, or at least the credentials imputing such skill and knowledge. And unlike real capital, these cannot be hoarded against hard times, preserved beyond the lifetime of an individual, or, of course, bequeathed... Whether the middle class looks down toward the realm of less, or up toward the realm of more, there is the fear, always, of falling.[42]

The connection of this class structure to freedom can be seen more clearly if we consider a favorite argument of Friedman's that regardless of the level of wealth concentration, the market allows for what he calls "proportional representation":

> ... the role of the market... is that it permits unanimity without conformity; that it is a system of effectively proportional representation... I cannot get the amount of national defense

I want and you, a different amount. With respect to such indivisible matters we can discuss, and argue, and vote. But having decided, we must conform.[43]

Friedman clearly glosses over some major problems here, which are brought forward thoughtfully by radical Left economist Robin Hahnel:

> It is not one person one vote, but one dollar one vote in the market place. Some claim this as a virtue: If I have a particularly strong preference for a good I can cast more dollar ballots to reflect the intensity of my desire... But, *there is something wrong when people have vastly different numbers of dollar ballots to cast in market elections.* Few would hold up as a paragon of freedom a political election in which some were permitted to vote thousands of times and others were permitted to vote only once, or not at all. But this is exactly the kind of freedom the market provides. Those with more income have a greater impact on what suppliers in markets will be signaled to provide than those with less income, which explains why 'market freedom' often leads to outcomes we know do not reflect what most people want... the intensity of people's desires for basic healthcare is higher than the intensity of desires for plastic surgery as well. But those voting for plastic surgery have many more votes to cast for even their less pressing desires than most voting for basic healthcare have even for life and death needs.[44]

So the modern class structures are a major impediment to real freedom, since the resources locked up in the portfolios of the owning class give them power and are kept from being freely used to express the basic requirements of the great majority. Unless, of course, the majority really does want shallow rich people to get butt-lifts.

On the other hand, the daily reality for those lowest on the global class structure is quickly summarized by the highly respected Indian economist Amartya Sen, who wrote in his influential *Poverty and Famines* that "Starvation is the characteristic of some people not *having* enough food to eat. It is not the characteristic of there *being* not enough food to eat. While the latter can be a cause of the former, it is but one of many *possible* causes."[45] Including the cause of being so abjectly poor that food is unaffordable, even if it is abundant for those higher in the class system—their enormous allowances express more desire for food than the desperate pleas but tiny incomes of the global poor. But for libertarian thinkers like Friedman and Hayek, who insist it's best to confine ourselves to negative freedom, starving people have no particular positive freedom or right to any surplus food.

A final genre of money's ability to grant more (hegemonic) freedom was described by columnist Russell Baker, who wrote:

> There are plenty of rich men who have no yachts and others who have no Picassos. Many of the rich have no winter homes in the South and there are a large number with no summer homes in the North. Many more have no private jets of their own, and a surprising number do not even have a chalet in the Alps. Every last one of them, however, has a lawyer... The man who has a lawyer working for him full time, year in and year out, is rich and, almost certainly, bound to get richer. What we have here is a class structure defined by degree of access to the law.[46]

Among the freedoms granted by enormous fortunes, is freedom from having to say you're sorry.

To the Bigger Go the Spoils

Having considered money's muscle, it's time to look at how markets really work. Capitalism is based on a market economy, in which decisions about what goods to produce and consume are made by consumers and producers, buying and selling from one another. The Friedmans wrote in *Free to Choose* that in a free market, "If one storekeeper offers you goods of lower quality or of higher price than another, you're not going to continue to patronize his store. If he buys goods to sell that don't serve your needs, you're not going to buy them... You are free to choose."[47] This picture is at the very heart of the modern conservative and libertarian worldview, and it's pretty laughable.

This picture of freedom to choose among many companies' products assumes that there *are* many different companies from which to buy. This market setting, with plenty of alternatives for consumers, is often called a *competitive* market in economic jargon, meaning it has many competing companies, which themselves must be small relative to the overall market. Friedman in *Capitalism and Freedom* wrote that "Of course, competition is an ideal type... as I have studied economic activities in the United States, I have become increasingly impressed with how wide is the range of problems and industries for which it is appropriate to treat the economy as if it were competitive."[48]

However, markets may become less competitive over time through a process called "concentration"—the tendency for smaller firms to get bought up or beaten down by the bigger firms. This can lead to a full "monopoly," where a single giant company supplies the entire market, or a lesser degree of monopoly called "oligopoly," where a market is dominated by just a few very large firms. Friedman calls monopoly one of "the most difficult problems" that can arise in an economy, explaining that monopolists have "control" of an industry and can "determine significantly the terms on which other individuals shall have access to it." This kind of control is called "market power"— the social, economic and political influence of giant companies. Concentrated market structures, like oligopoly, allow big firms to gain different levels of market power, and sometimes to work together and wield even more authority.[49]

Friedman claims "By removing the organization of economic activity from the control of political authority, the market eliminates this source of coercive power... Economic power can be widely dispersed. There is no law of conservation which forces the growth of new centers of economic strength to be at the expense of existing centers."[50] Later, he insists "The most important fact about enterprise monopoly is its relative unimportance from the point of view of the economy as a whole."[51]

This baked-in denial crosses mainstream political lines. For example, Paul Krugman, one of the most respected liberal economists in the US, concludes his textbook's chapter on the subject by observing "across industries, oligopoly is far more common than either perfect competition or monopoly." Yet, he feels the reflexive assumption of free market competition is still justified, because often "the industry behaves 'almost' as if it were perfectly competitive."[52]

Some of the best research on the subject of these "market structures" is by author Barry Lynn, whose outstanding book *Cornered* documents the concentration of market after market, often hidden from our view by maintaining independent brand names even after being bought by giant conglomerates. For example, nine of the ten best-selling brands of bottled water are sold by three firms—Pepsi, Coke and Nestle.[53] Looking at eyeglasses, "LensCrafters, Sears Optical, and Sunglass Hut are all owned by the same company, the Italian eyewear conglomerate Luxottica."[54] Turning to the working man's beer, "all the microbreweries and brew pubs together accounted for less than 4 percent" of the total, while "among the industrial brewers, consolidation never stopped... With the merger in 2007 of Miller and Coors, under the direction of South African Breweries (SAB), and the takeover in 2008 of Anheuser-Busch by InBev, the United States... was basically reduced to reliance on a world-bestriding beer duopoly, run not out of Milwaukee or St. Louis but out of Leuven, Belgium, and Johannesburg, South Africa."[55] And now, just Belgium, since in 2015 AB InBev itself announced a $108 billion purchase of SAB Miller.[56]

Scholars of monopoly and market concentration have found that the degree of consolidation depends on the peculiarities of different markets, with some industries having several factors pushing for oligopoly and market power, while other markets may remain decentralized. One major driver is the economy of scale. An economy of scale occurs when a company's per-unit costs decrease as it produces more goods, usually because the firm operates in an industry with large up-front expenses, like manufacturing. If a firm invests $1 billion in a cell phone factory and ends up producing just phones, each unit will cost $1 million before labor and materials expenses. But if the factory instead produces 10 million phones over its lifetime, the cost of capital per unit drops to $100 each.

These incentives have been present since the Industrial Revolution; although conservative economists prefer not to recognize their importance. Hayek considered market concentration to be "exaggerated"[57] and he held the government to be usually responsible for it. He dismissed the argument that "technological changes have made competition impossible in a constantly increasing number of fields," claiming "This belief derives mainly from the Marxist doctrine of the concentration of industry."[58]

But economists with an interest in the opinions of actual business people have found they frequently report scale economies. Mid-century US economists Wilford Eiteman and Glenn Guthrie directly surveyed heads of manufacturing corporations, with striking results—only about 5 percent of surveyed firms reported the rising costs conventionally expected by economists, while 94 percent reported scale economies of different types.[59] The highly respected Harvard business professor Alfred Chandler wrote in his meticulous business history *Scale and Scope* that as industries grew:

> Production units achieved much greater economies of scale... Therefore large plants operating at their 'minimum efficient scale' (the scale of operation necessary to reach the lowest cost per unit) had an impressive cost advantage over smaller plants that did not reach that scale... In many industries the throughput of plants of that scale was so high that a small number of them could meet the existing national and even global demand. The structure of these industries quickly became oligopolistic... In many instances the first company to build a plant of minimum efficient scale and to recruit the essential management team remained the leader in its industry for decades.[60]

Chandler also appreciated that these scale efficiencies meant "market power." He points to an incredible letter written among executive staff of the great DuPont chemical empire, suggesting that if the firm gained:

> ... an absolute monopoly in the field, it would not pay us... The demand of the country for [gun]powder is variable. If we owned all therefore when slack times came we would have to curtail product to the extent of diminished demands. If on the other hand we control only 60% of it all and made the 60% cheaper than others, when slack times came we could still keep our capital employed to the full and our product to the maximum by taking from the other 40% what was needed for this purpose.[61]

From a very different perspective, the radical historian Douglas Dowd agreed, observing that large-scale industrial technology made it "*necessary* for business firms to enlarge... *and* possible to increase their profits by their ability to control their markets."[62] The unorthodox Australian economist Steve Keen confirmed "increasing returns to scale mean that the perfectly competitive market is unstable: it will, in time, break down" into oligopoly or monopoly.[63] This is an impressive level of agreement among industrialists, eminent business historians and radical analysts. In the face of this very broad consensus, Mises' and Hayek's claim that concentration is purely a "Marxist doctrine" doesn't pass the laugh test.

Beside scale economies, another driver of market concentration emerges among major merchant companies, those that buy goods from manufacturers and sell them to consumers. These "trading monopolies" arise when a merchant firm or retailer gains such a large share of a consumer goods marketplace that they become indispensable to manufacturers and wholesalers, to whom they can dictate terms and arm-wrestle over prices. Today, there are two principal US merchant monopolists—Wal-Mart and Amazon.

The real gravity of Wal-Mart lies in its power, technically called "monopsony"—a firm that has power not only for much of what it sells, but also for what it *buys*. Consider Pankaj Ghemawat's analysis of the firm in the prestigious *Harvard Business Review*:

Size advantages exist because markets are finite... Wal-Mart, the discount merchandiser, illustrates the power of local and regional scale economies. Historically, it focused on small Sunbelt towns that its competitors had neglected. Most of these towns could not support two discounters, so once Wal-Mart made a long-lived, largely unrecoverable investment to service such a town, it gained a local monopoly. The company reinforced this advantage by wrapping its stores in concentric rings around regional distribution centers. By the time competitors realized that this policy cut distribution costs in half, Wal-Mart had preempted enough store sites to render competing regional warehouses unviable. Now you know why Sam Walton is one of the richest men in America.[64]

And why, when Walton died, his four kids each became one of the ten richest Americans.

The power of Small-Mart's monopsony is enough for it reorganize and oligopolize whole industries through its "category captain" system. As company historian Charles Fishman put it, "Wal-Mart retains the power in the relationship," since Wal-Mart buys 20 percent or more of many manufacturers' output.[65] Barry Lynn observes that "Free-market Utopians have long decried government industrial policy because it puts into the hands of bureaucrats and politicians the power to determine which firms 'win' and which 'lose.' Wal-Mart picks winners and losers every day."[66] Hayek's argument was that government "central planning" is the Road to Serfdom since it represses diverse markets. But private sector powermongers are apparently less scary.

Meanwhile, Amazon is becoming the online Wal-Mart, for a start clearing a third of US book sales, a hugely influential position when the big bookstore chains are bankrupt or close to it, and independents now rare. As Paul Constant of the Seattle *Stranger* put it, "We now live in an America dotted with 'bookstore deserts,' where people would have to drive for hours, maybe even a full day, to browse the stacks at an Amazon competitor."[67]

Businessweek journalist Brad Stone wrote that:

Amazon had an easy way to demonstrate its market power. When a publisher did not capitulate and the company shut off the recommendation algorithms for its books, the publisher's sales usually fell by as much as 40 percent... Bezos kept pushing for more. He asked [an employee] to exact better terms from the smallest publishers, who would go out of business if it weren't for the steady sales of their back catalogs on Amazon.

Amazon's libertarian CEO Jeff Bezos called this "the Gazelle Project," meaning "Amazon should approach these small publishers the way a cheetah would pursue a sickly gazelle." But soon "Amazon's lawyers heard about the name and insisted it be changed to the less incendiary Small Publisher Program."[68] Amazon's more common move was simply the mere "threat of decreased promotion on the site," a negotiating tactic Amazon called "Pay to Play. Once again, Amazon's lawyers caught wind of this and renamed the program Vendor Realignment."[69]

These tactics have also worked against other major firms, like Macmillan and Time-Warner.[70] The business world is watching as "The retailer's power in the book industry... has prompted publishers to move toward consolidation as they look to fortify their own negotiating positions by adding heft and larger inventory."[71] Once again, free competition it ain't. Prices are often set by this kind of corporate pissing contest rather than the "invisible hand" of efficiency.

Lynn observes that online commerce actually has an especially strong concentration drive:

Precisely because the Internet eliminates the "tyranny" of locality, it eliminates most of the physical obstacles to centralization, such as the price of real estate. The result is consolidation beyond anything we have ever seen in the physical world, often in the form of a single superdominant entity—Netflix, Amazon, iTunes—that also tends to enjoy real cost advantages over real-world rivals.[72]

Notably, Amazon founder Jeff Bezos is himself a libertarian (while his cofounder Nick Hanauer says he fears "pitchforks" coming for his "fellow zillionaires").[73] So Bezos claims to believe in a market with many firms and scrappy competition, but once his market dominance is established the firm shows its true colors, arm-wrestling with other corporate titans and towering over "sickly gazelles." Thus, libertarianism is refuted by another of its own powerful adherents.

A final form of market concentration (whether it leads to oligopoly or a full monopoly) is found in markets that involve networks, such as air travel, Internet service or electric power. These markets have an inherent tendency to concentrate, since the value of a network is increased the larger it gets—clearly, an airline with gates in a hundred cities is worth more than one with gates in ten cities, and a social media network is worth more as it connects more users.

But even these cases don't move Friedman:

Railroads in the United States are an excellent example. A large degree of monopoly in railroads was perhaps inevitable on technical grounds in the nineteenth century... But conditions have changed. The emergence of road and air transport has reduced the monopoly element in railroads to negligible proportions... If railroads had never been subjected to regulation in the United States, it is nearly certain that by now transportation, including railroads, would be a highly competitive industry with little or no remaining monopoly elements.[74]

Friedman got his wish when the rail freight industry was deregulated in 1980 with the Staggers Rail Act, which removed limits on shipping charges, and related legislation exempted the rails from anti-monopoly laws.

Friedman thought this would unleash new competition,

but as often happens, when regulation was loosened the "Age of Friedman" seemed to be a rerun of the nineteenth century's Gilded Age. As *Fortune* magazine describes complaints against the rail corporations:

> The central charge is one that would've been familiar to Rockefeller: monopoly power. Since freight railroads were deregulated in 1980, the number of large, so-called Class I railroads has shrunk from 40 to seven. In truth, there are only four that matter: CSX and Norfolk Southern in the East, Union Pacific and Burlington Northern Santa Fe in the West. These four superpowers now take in more than 90% of the industry's revenue... An estimated one-third of shippers have access to only one railroad.[75]

And so free-market economics fails yet another test. Conservatives to this day blame dissatisfaction with capitalism on government regulation, saying that if only it were abolished we would "nearly certainly" see "a highly competitive industry." But when regulations fall away here on planet Earth, networks and big upfront costs make an outcome of "four superpowers" almost inevitable. Irony loves company!

Industries like these, with network effects and also giant upfront costs creating scale economies, are often referred to as "natural monopolies" — their efficiencies are strong enough to make a monopolist more efficient than multiple firms. Often, cases like these are considered to be the ones with the best case for running the industry through a public body, or for at least strong regulation, since market competition is especially clearly not in effect. And while the Right recognizes the issue, even here they prefer that markets run unimpeded, even if it means a monopoly. Friedman states: "When technical conditions make a monopoly the natural outcome of competitive market forces, there are only three alternatives that seem available: private monopoly, public monopoly, or public regulation. All three are bad so we must choose among evils... Having learned from both, I reluctantly conclude that, if tolerable, private monopoly may be the least of the evils."[76] In fact, he later specifies that even government oversight is too much, urging "private unregulated monopoly,"[77] like Standard Oil in the early days.

The emerging future of monopoly was projected by *The Wall Street Journal*'s own headline covering the major online companies, "Giants Tighten Grip on Internet Economy," and illustrated with a gigantic flying saucer covered in corporate logos, apparently beaming individuals aboard.[78] It plainly reported that "the Internet economy is powered by an infrastructure... controlled by a small handful of tech giants" and described Google, Microsoft, Apple, Amazon and Facebook as "established companies [that] dominate in essential services that both fuel and extract value from the rising digital economy." Their centrality to the very functioning of the Internet means "ecosystems" are gradually built around these corporate nodes, so that "Anyone building a brand, for example, can't ignore Facebook's highly engaged daily audience of 1 billion. Anyone starting a business needs to make sure they can be found on Google. Anyone with goods to sell wants Amazon to carry them." Similar status applies for mobile apps, music and video.

Google's search monopoly has an especially crucial role, one which net neutrality pioneer Tim Wu called "the Web's great switch" for exploring information, a hugely important position.[79] *The New York Times*' sympathetic technophile calls these firms the "Frightful Five" that "lord over all that happens in tech" and are "better insulated against surprising competition from upstarts." At turns rivals and partners, they are "inescapable," "central to just about everything we do with computers," and together they "form a gilded mesh blanketing the entire economy."[80] Less floridly, they own the "platforms" — the basic systems and network hubs increasingly relied on by the rest of the economy, including for social interaction.

However, many liberals and some conservatives suggest that all this talk about "economic power" is overblown, since "antitrust" law outlaws any "restraint of trade," like powerful monopolies. Liberals like Lynn, who would rather see capitalism preserved but regulated to take the edges off, claim that antitrust law puts "checks on the autocratic power of the corporate managers and the labor bosses."[81]

This faith has been shaken by the aggressive weakening of antitrust law over the last forty years, since it relies on a representative government, standing up to concentrated capital. This problem will be examined in Chapter 3, but for now radical economist Edward Herman notes "Antitrust has gone through cycles," with the last "cycle" beginning in the Reagan administration, which "aggressively dismantled antitrust, imposing drastic cuts in budgets and manpower, installing officials hostile to the antitrust mission, and failing to enforce the laws."[82]

The business press observed at the time that "Stressing deregulation, the Reagan Administration appears likely to aim at a more relaxed and flexible approach to antitrust policy," with the new head of the program favoring "an antitrust policy based on efficiency considerations."[83] So if corporations can convince the Justice Department it will save money by merging, the division may sign off on it, regardless of its effects on market power. This is why antitrust often allows absurdly anticompetitive mergers, like that in 2006 between the appliance makers Maytag and Whirlpool, with its "combined market share of 50 to 80 percent for washers, dryers and dishwashers, with refrigerators not far behind."[84] The EU and other nations have experienced broadly similar trends.

But enforced or not, the inherent limits of antitrust policy's ability to fix the fundamental problem of market concentration are given by Harvard's Chandler. He comments "the existence of the Sherman Act discouraged monopoly in industries where integration and concentration had already occurred. It helped to create oligopoly where monopoly existed and to prevent oligopoly from becoming monopoly."[85] In other words, antitrust (when it was enforced) prevented full monopoly but left gigantic networks of vertically integrated firms in place to dominate the marketplace.

When briefly mentioning these issues, Friedman remarks,

"What about the danger of monopoly that led to the antitrust laws? That is a real danger. The most effective way to counter it is not through a bigger antitrust division at the Department of Justice or a larger budget for the Federal Trade Commission, but through removing existing barriers to international trade. That would permit competition from all over the world to be even more effective than it is now in undermining monopoly at home."[86]

Regrettably for Friedman's breezy dismissal of the issue, many oligopolies and monopolies are today global in their scope.

Consider Exxon-Mobil. After Rockefeller's free-market monopoly Standard Oil was broken up into a regional oligopoly under antitrust action in 1911, several of its pieces rejoined in the "relaxed antitrust" era of the Age of Friedman. This created colossal firms like Exxon, and indeed in this industry the US government even encouraged this as a lever of US power over world energy markets. *Businessweek* memorably described the company's CEO as "The Man," commenting ironically "The Man is not a head of state, but the distinction is academic." [87] It notes "the plush senior management suite at Exxon's headquarters is known within the industry as the 'God Pod,'" typical of "the sovereign state of Exxon, accustomed as it is to using its superior technology and financial muscle to dominate not only rival companies but whole countries." The business writers call Exxon "capitalism exemplified." Despite Friedman's sweet hopes, the global market is not big enough to make any firm into small player.

So just how concentrated is, for example, the US economy? The Concentration Ratios calculated by the Economic Census in the US Commerce Department are quite incomplete, but are the best record we have. Even their limited figures are striking, with the 2012 census indicating that the eight largest pet food firms produce over 80 percent of the US total (by share of value added, generally proportionate to production); the biggest four snack food firms produced more than half the US total; the eight biggest coffee and tea companies produce 70 percent of the full output; the four biggest book publishers earn more than 40 percent of the industry's total revenue; and the eight largest software publishers write enough code to earn almost half the market income.[88] And while the global record differs in detail, the overall trend is clear. The data, though problematic and limited, shows a clear pattern of concentration across many crucial industries.

Indeed, the loyalty of the Right and today's "libertarians" to their view of competitive markets and their alleged "free association" is almost touching, considering the towering heights of power the early tycoons reached before the mild threat of antitrust was created. Consider the nineteenth century's "Gilded Age," the time of purest, nonregulated and lightly-taxed *laissez-faire* capitalism in the US and Europe. That era didn't see a flourishing of enduringly competitive markets with "free to choose" consumers and workers, but instead a very consistent concentration drive toward oligopoly or worse—Standard Oil, American Tobacco and US Steel are classic free-market monopolies. The early railroad kingpin Cornelius Vanderbilt remarked when facing a legal obstacle, "What do I care about the law? Hain't I got power?"[89] Likewise, Wall Street kingpin JP Morgan arranged huge horizontal and vertical mergers among corporations across the economy, giving rise to a whole series of monopolies and trusts that were "Morganized" by the powerful figure, including the colossal US Steel monopoly.

So, after this review of the record of market concentration, intermittent government regulation and business power, what is left of the libertarian idea of "free to choose?" The answer is given by Rothbard. "If consumer demand had really justified more competitors or more of the product or a greater variety of products, then entrepreneurs would have seized the opportunity to profit by satisfying this demand. The fact that this is not being done in any given case demonstrates that no such unsatisfied consumer demand exists."[90] So no level of monopoly can *possibly* deface our free-market doctrine, revealing the right-wing intellectual tradition as a disgraceful fraud and a sickening waste. While governments do indeed often promote giant semi-monopolist corporations as "national champions," the point libertarians sweep under the rug is that the market is quite capable of producing towering corporations with full monopoly power all by itself.

George Orwell, the globally celebrated journalist and critic of the totalitarianism of the Soviet Union, himself reviewed Hayek's book *The Road to Serfdom* for the London *Observer* in 1944. He agreed with Hayek's claim, as Orwell put it, that "collectivism is not inherently democratic," an insight born of Orwell's own evolving socialist positions (see Chapter 5). But his torpedoing of the core flaw of Hayek's arguments was simple:

> But he does not see, or will not admit, that a return to 'free' competition means for the great mass of people a tyranny probably worse, because more irresponsible, than that of the State. The trouble with competitions is that somebody wins them. Professor Hayek denies that free capitalism necessarily leads to monopoly, but in practice that is where it has led.[91]

But apparently Wal-Mart's "local monopolies" and tycoons laughing at the law aren't too impressive to libertarian and conservative economists, who are, after all, Free To Choose to ignore reality. But this happy view of market concentration contrasts with the very different way economists view labor concentration.

Labor's Loves Lost

By now, we've reviewed the strong concentration of capital ownership, both in household fortunes as well as market consolidation. But what about labor? The Right's take on the freedom of the labor market is that it leaves us free to choose among multiple uses for our labor, protecting you from power plays by a tyrannical boss.

> The most reliable and effective protection for most workers is provided by the existence of many employers... The employers who protect a worker are those who would like to hire him. Their demand for his services makes it in the self-interest of his own employer to pay him the full value of his work. If his own employer doesn't, someone else may be ready to do so. Competition for his services—that is the worker's real protection.[92]

The first serious problem with these rosy reviews of the market is that after the previous section, it must be admitted that the "many employers" the Friedmans are expecting may never arrive to the job fair. And they do quietly concede that "Two classes or workers are not protected by anyone: workers who have only one possible employer, and workers who have no possible employer,"[93] which makes consolidation and outsourcing very relevant for freedom.

The second great problem is that, fundamentally, people are

in fact not commodities. A seller of non-perishable goods can store them until market conditions are favorable. This patience is unavailable for owners of mere labor power, who stubbornly require food and water at regular intervals. The kid cannot skip eating this quarter and eat more next quarter instead. Treating labor as an asset priced by supply and demand, like toasters or toothbrushes, is a gross insult to the human spirit and indeed, is responsible for some of the gravest crimes committed against humanity in our history.

A further problem is that this traditional claim that the labor market is "free" is based on another assumption, that if you don't find an employer you want to work for, you can just produce goods on your own. Friedman states: "Since the household always has the alternative of producing directly for itself, it need not enter into any exchange unless it benefits from it. Hence, no exchange will take place unless both parties do benefit from it."[94] This would indeed grant a good deal of freedom to the man on the street, but "producing for itself" implies access to productive resources, including what we call "capital," which as we've seen is so highly concentrated that a very large part of global society has essentially none. This means that since we have no "positive freedom" to use or decide on how to use the capital stock, the typical working person is also left with diminished "negative freedom," since employers who own the concentrated capital have dramatic power over employees in the market.

Ultimately, these problems mean that the workforce is constantly tempted to organize, in order to gain some collective power of its own to set against the weight of giant organized companies. The main form of workforce organization is the labor union, where workers organize into bargaining units that can negotiate with companies on more equal terms. Despite reliably hostile media coverage (see Chapter 2), unions remain popular among the global workforce, with worker surveys and even *Businessweek* reporting that Americans say in rising numbers that they would like to form a union in their workplace.[95] More recently, the Gallup polling agency found in 2015 that Americans' approval of labor unions had reached nearly six in ten, yet more than half expected them to continue to weaken.[96] And labor's loves, the major gains won by the movement, have also turned out be pretty enduringly popular: the common observance of a "weekend" when many workers have regular time off, the eight-hour day for much of the workforce and child labor laws that encourage kids to go to school rather than competing with adults for jobs.

The reasons for this generally popular view of unionizing are explained by many sources, including by civil rights hero Martin Luther King Jr, who in his brief but historic career made allies of labor and spoke often at meetings of labor union locals:

> The labor movement was the principal force that transformed misery and despair into hope and progress. Out of its bold struggles, economic and social reform gave birth to unemployment insurance, old-age pensions, government relief for the destitute, and, above all, new wage levels that meant not mere survival but a tolerable life. The captains of industry did not lead this transformation; they resisted it until they were overcome.[97]

Indeed, King said the labor movement and the civil rights movement both fought "the economic and political power structure."

But most importantly for the main points of this chapter, King told an AFL conference in 1961 that the labor movement arose because before it the working man "was hired and fired by economic despots whose power over him decreed his life or death... Those who in the second half of the nineteenth century could not tolerate organized labor have had a rebirth of power and seek to regain the despotism of that era while retaining the wealth and privileges of the twentieth century."[98] A "despot" is an entity with supreme power, something very far from the traditional picture of "many holders" of money that the Right promotes. King criticized "the tragic inequalities of an economic system which takes necessities from the masses to give luxuries to the classes" and in one of his final speeches, he celebrated the power of organized people to stand up to governments and concentrated capital:

> We can all get more together than we can apart; we can get more organized together than we can apart. And this is the way we gain power. Power is the ability to achieve purpose, power is the ability to affect change, and we need power. What is power? Walter Reuther said once that "power is the ability of a labor union like UAW to make the most powerful corporation in the world—General Motors—say yes when it wants to say no."[99]

Few are aware that King was assassinated while supporting a Memphis, Tennessee labor action, supporting city garbage men who were on strike for recognition of their union. King often called the opponents of labor and civil rights "reactionary,"[100] a derogatory term for the Right's political views, implying they favor static tradition or a return to the past. This could quite easily apply to Hayek, Friedman and many of today's libertarians and their hankering for a return to the Gilded Age.

Despite the relative popularity of unions, the institution has also been in steady decline for decades. The Economic Policy Institute finds "union density," the proportion of the national labor force that's represented by a union collective bargaining contract, has fallen from 26.7 percent in 1973 to 13.0 percent in 2011.[101] The *Harvard Business Review* also observes that "Labor is on its own politically in America in the 21st century,"[102] a fact we'll come back to in Chapter 3. It may be confusing that unions have declined even as their popularity has largely held up and the solution to the puzzle is labor repression. Since the era of early capitalism, labor has faced major obstacles to solidarity, with workers split along racial, class, gender and occupational lines. Much worse, striking workers were often violently attacked by hired company thugs like the Pinkertons, who outright massacred strikers in episodes like the Homestead steel strike. Open anti-labor violence mostly ended in the developed world following the late nineteenth century, but remains quite common in the Third World (see Chapter 5).

In the developed world, more modern methods are based on misinformation and bullying, as when *Businessweek* reports that worker surveys had indicated a gradually rising willingness to join a labor union, but found:

... heightened corporate power has checked union growth... Unionization elections are typically so lopsided that most unions have all but given up on them. Most employers pull out the stops when labor organizers appear, using everything from mandatory antiunion meetings to staged videos showing alleged union thugs beating workers, backed by streams of leaflets and letters to workers' homes. While most of these tactics are legal, companies also illegally fire union supporters in 25 percent of all elections.[103]

These moves have left organized labor a dramatically reduced player in the US economy.

However, the economists on the Right have more scalding antagonism for unions than for any other social institution, even the state itself. Unlike their treatment of the market, where the power of huge corporate empires is reliably minimized or called "inappropriate" to discuss, with labor organization the treatment is very different. In *Free to Choose*, the Friedmans cut straight to the issue that evaded them while looking at the business world—they start with a section directly titled "The Source of Union Power," which concludes that unions "enforce a high wage rate" with government action or through "violence or the threat of violence: threatening to destroy the property of employers, or to beat them up.[104]

Libertarians can very reliably be counted on to immediately counter any mention of "corporate power" or "economic power" with the demand, "Well what about labor power?" Labor power still exists today, but the influence of organized labor has flagged along with its density numbers. Trying to put equal blame on corporate empires and labor unions is pretty ridiculous, similar to blaming in equal measure the business world and the churches, or the organized fraternal societies like the Rotary Club. All these institutions have some influence and some even have a measure of social power, but compared to the colossal corporate concentration numbers in the last section, their weight is small potatoes.

This kind of naked defense of power is even more glaring if we take up the Right's view of trade organizations, a very prominent part of the economic scene, as Robert Brady observed in his fine but almost-unknown book *Business As a System of Power*. For example, a "Resolution on trade associations" adopted by the powerful National Association of Manufacturers (NAM) "heartily approves the plan of organizing each industry in the country in a representative national trade association" and hoped "every dealer, jobber, manufacturer, and producer of raw materials should be a member."[105] However, NAM's most core program was to resist *worker* organization, as Brady observes: "except for certain short intervals, its overshadowing interest has been in labor relations. A common interest in opposing organized labor has served to hold the membership together, to dominate the motives in organizing and perfecting the machinery" of organization.[106]

This is oddly similar to Hayek's view of the issue: "It is

merely a play upon words to speak of the 'power collectively exercised by private boards of directors' so long as they do not combine to concerted action—which would, of course, mean the end of competition and the creation of a planned economy."[107] But that's the point—they *do* combine for concerted action, both by merging into larger conglomerates and by organizing into industry associations. Rather than the "planned economy" of socialism that haunts Hayek's dreams, it is corporate monopoly and oligopoly, and their industrial organizations, that are the main source of today's central planning. Brady concludes, "The real significance of such concentration is found less in the exercise of direct monopolistic powers than in the position of leadership of the giant concerns in their respective fields... by such devices as 'price leadership,' [or] 'sharing the market,'" in line with Chandler's analysis above.[108]

Here, in the face of the Right's contempt for organized labor and its selective blindness concerning organized capital, we should remember one of their idols, Adam Smith. Smith is commonly considered the father of the economics discipline, and among conservative economists like Friedman and Hayek he's an especially crucial figure. But Smith's picture of the capital-labor dynamic depends fundamentally on the question of organization (or as he wrote, "combination") and deserves to be quoted at length:

The workmen desire to get as much, the masters to give as little as possible. The former are disposed to combine in order to raise, the latter in order to lower the wages of labour. It is not, however, difficult to foresee which of the two parties must, upon all ordinary occasions, have the advantage in the dispute, and force the other into a compliance with their terms. The masters, being fewer in number, can combine more easily; and the law, besides, authorizes, or at least does not prohibit their combinations, while it prohibits those of the workmen. We have no acts of parliament against combining to lower the price of work; but many against combining to raise it. In all such disputes the masters can hold out much longer. A landlord, a farmer, a master manufacturer, or merchant, though they did not employ a single workman, could generally live a year or two upon the stocks they have already acquired. Many workmen could not subsist a week, few could subsist a month, and scarce any a year without employment. In the long-run the workman may be as necessary to his master as his master is to him; but the necessity is not so immediate.

We rarely hear, it has been said, of the combinations of masters; though frequently of those of workmen. But whoever imagines, upon this account, that masters rarely combine, is as ignorant of the world as of the subject... Such combinations, however, are frequently resisted by a contrary defensive combination of the workmen; who sometimes too, without any provocation of this kind, combine of their own accord to raise the price of their labour... But whether their combinations be offensive or defensive, they are always abundantly heard of.[109]

Smith, who again is considered a heroic intellectual figure across numerous economic schools, describes a labor market that is basically an organization-off: which side can best organize and outmaneuver the other drives the outcome, and in most cases business has the edge. In fact, this is a simple description of class conflict.

Hayek hopes he "will not be suspected of any tenderness toward the capitalists if he stresses here that it would nevertheless be a mistake to put the blame for the modern movement toward monopoly exclusively or mainly on that class. Their propensity in this direction is neither new nor would it by itself be likely to become a formidable power."[110] Similarly, Friedman says in

Capitalism and Freedom: "While there seems not to have been any upward trend in the importance of enterprise monopoly over the past half-century, there certainly has been in the importance of labor monopoly." Obviously, based on the numbers in the Age of Friedman, the opposite is true.

This consistent pattern frankly reveals that a number of quite respected, Nobel Prize-winning conservative economists, including Friedman and Hayek, are intellectual opportunists. By coincidence, their analysis has bottomless contempt for organized labor (even on its now-small scale), but the giant crimes of the enormously greater power of organized capital are studiously ignored. This puts Friedman and Hayek closer to other figures who have used their formidable intellects to defend other cruel power systems. We have little respect today for intellectual supporters of slavery, of the "divine right" of kings and the feudal system, of the Nazi or Soviet states, or other tyrannical powermongers. Today's "libertarian" intellectuals take their place in a long tradition of *defense of power*, a parade of shame stretching back to the ancient priests who defended the righteousness of early kings with fine-sounding words.

There is an exception to this pathetically opportunistic judgment of power systems—these right-wing kingpins will recognize corporate power *if* labor is involved and can take the fall. Hayek claimed "the impetus of the movement toward totalitarianism comes mainly from the two great vested interests: organized capital and organized labor. Probably the greatest menace of all is the fact that the policies of these two most powerful groups point in the same direction."[111] After the previous section and Smith's analysis earlier, the claim that the interests of labor and "the capitalist class" often "point the same direction" is pretty laughable. A more historically accurate picture comes from the Gilded Age railroad developer and financier Jay Gould, who said simply "I can hire one-half of the working class to kill the other half."[112]

Consider the prominent recent case of collusion in Silicon Valley, in which some of the biggest firms in the high-tech economy were caught conspiring to keep down the wages of their software engineers. The "tech giants" were caught on email agreeing not to "recruit," or try to hire, engineers from one another, in order to restrain their salaries.[113] Collusion is messy and after a Google recruiter contacted an Apple employee, CEO Steve Jobs wrote to Google's CEO Eric Schmidt in a bullying tone, and Schmidt promptly informed Jobs the employee would be "fired within the hour."[114] *The Wall Street Journal* reports Jobs then forwarded that email to other Apple execs "and added a smiley face."[115]

The sharpest lesson of the affair came from economist Dean Baker:

> The classic libertarian view of the market is that we have a huge number of people in the market actively competing to buy and sell goods and services... However, the Silicon Valley non-compete agreements show that this is not how the tech billionaires believe the market really works. This is just a story they peddle to children and gullible reporters... The fact that the Silicon Valley honchos took the time to negotiate and presumably enforce these non-compete agreements was because they did not think that there were enough competitors to hire away their workers. They believed that they had enough weight on the buy-side of the market for software engineers that if they agreed not to compete for workers, they could keep their wages down.[116]

In the end, it's a picture of lopsided power: the giant stature of immortal, powermongering corporations owned by the richest families versus hard-to-organize hungry human beings whose unions have been in decline for several decades now. But this major imbalance of negotiating leverage originates in the grossly skewed concentration of wealth and the time has come to take a look at the very different lives led by people in the different classes.

No Man is an Island, But He Can Buy One

After this analysis of classes, market power and the decline of labor, we can take a moment to survey the actual world created by these economic processes. After all, day-to-day life is a story of lived experiences, not just aggregate numbers. The wild divergence of these class realities is most striking in the area of housing. Housing is of course extremely important for the world majority, not just for its inherent utility as basic shelter, but also as the principle investment of the developed world's middle class. But millions of Americans have borrowed heavily against their homes, in addition to those who lost their homes to foreclosure during and after the 2008 crisis, with the EPI concluding that "creditors, including banks, own far more of the nation's housing stock than people do."[117]

But for the owning class, the recent experience of housing volatility is dramatically different. Consider the most expensive neighborhoods of New York City, where a high-end property developer remarks "It's like a return to the Gilded Age," referring again to the late nineteenth century when low taxes, weak regulation and almost nonexistent unions meant a society close to pure capitalism. The Age of Friedman policies are bringing us gradually back to that era, even on the streets: "After spending decades doing duty as schools, embassies, consulates, nonprofit headquarters, apartment houses and the like... important and irreplaceable buildings" are advertised as "ripe for conversion to what they were in the beginning: beauteous, commodious and expensive single-family residences."[118] Or as *The New York Times* calls them, "Trophy townhouses."

But the rich have problems, too: Manhattan is notoriously

impossible for parking, so a new luxury development is offering parking spaces for $1 million apiece.[119] The rationale, as the developer puts it: "When someone is paying $50 million for an apartment, another $500,000 for the luxury of not walking a block or two and having your own spot, I guess it becomes a rounding error." Although it takes a regular American 20 years of work to pay for that rounding error. Or 113 for a regular Thai, or 625 years for the average Brazilian.

Besides the return of in-city mansions for the affluent and their cars, New York and London have also seen the growth of "poor doors." These are entrances to new luxury buildings, erected with a city requirement to include some affordable housing units for regular working people, in addition to "market rate" units that sell in the seven figures and up.[120] *The Guardian* describes a luxury London development where the main door opens to "luxury marble tiling and plush sofas, and a sign on the door alerts residents to the fact that the concierge is available. Round the back, the entrance to the affordable homes is a cream corridor, decorated only with grey mail boxes and a poster warning tenants that they are on CCTV and will be prosecuted if they cause any damage."[121] An agent for wealthy buyers is quoted saying that the purpose of the doors is "so the two social strata don't have to meet."[122]

The extra doors are also slightly ironic, since the more expensive neighborhoods have a high concentration of second or third apartments for globally affluent families or individuals, meaning they often go empty. *The Times* describes a tony street where "very few people come and go, because most of the apartment owners live someplace else... This very costly form of desolation means that some of the city's most expensive residential buildings stand mostly dark, lonesome and empty on the inside." Just like their owners! So while New York City has large numbers of homeless people die on its streets every winter, a condo tower in the Time Warner complex is "generally about 60 percent occupied, while those in the north tower are only about 30 percent occupied." A high social cost, not lost on those only moderately rich full-time residents who are, as *The Times* put it, "living in a deserted piggy bank."[123]

And even as their properties sit in empty silence, the top 1 percent indulges in hotel stays with bills to startle the most jaded observers. The trend is reviewed in *The Wall Street Journal* articles on elite suites around the world, including "bathrooms clad in honey-colored onyx and Skyros marble, with shelves lined in leather... a walk-in cellar and a spa suite... 21,000-square-foot suite has its own hair salon and movie theater... a two-story round library complete with a secret passageway."[124] The Ritz-Carlton Abu Dhabi's Royal Suite has a neighboring room for bodyguards. The New York Palace has its own massive space "which a Saudi prince spent $12 million refurbishing for a six-month stay some years back," which comes to about $2 million per prince-month.

However, nothing compares to Ralph Ellison's little place on the water—he recently bought a Hawaiian island. As *The Wall Street Journal* recounts, while it doesn't quite "feel real" to him, the Oracle founder and billionaire "owns nearly everything on the island, including many of the candy-colored plantation-style homes and apartments, one of the two grocery stores, the Four Seasons hotels and golf courses, the community center and pool, water company, movie theater, half the roads and some 88,000 acres of land."[125] The approving *Journal* acknowledges that the "local population" is "one whose economic future is heavily dependent on his decisions," but the billionaire's purchase of an airline to ferry out hyper-wealthy tourists from Honolulu makes it okay.

Beyond housing, conspicuous consumption takes on cruelly wasteful proportions, like $700 Aniversario cigars and $6000 handbags. These are eclipsed, though, by the high-end home tennis court at $55,000, the $330,000 yearling race horse and the $11 million personal Sikorsky helicopter, for flying into Manhattan to shop without sitting in traffic on Route 27 back to the Hamptons. These and many other owning-class necessities are compiled annually by *Forbes* in its "Cost of Living Extremely Well Index," sampling the budget demands of the wealthiest US households.[126] Family budget entries include $14,000 facelifts and $400,000 in annual yacht maintenance, a far cry from the working-class choice between Junior's college fund and keeping the heat on.

But the most revealing ruling class recreation is philanthropy. This habit is one of the most common defenses of the ruling class: while these figures may wield enormous fortunes, they are generous and share the wealth through donations to important charities, these days usually through creating an endowed foundation. The Friedmans claim in *Free to Choose* that plutocrats are getting a bum rap: "The charge of heartlessness, epitomized in the remark that William H. Vanderbilt, a railroad tycoon, is said to have made to an inquiring reporter, 'The public be damned,' is belied by the flowering of charitable activity in the United States in the nineteenth century."[127] More generally, "private fortunes were largely devoted in the end to the benefit of society."[128]

And, indeed, the amounts of money involved are impressive, as the nineteenth-century free-market monopolists Carnegie and Rockefeller gave away billions (in today's dollars) to fight disease, and build libraries and churches.[129] But, in fact, this dramatic philanthropy is another manifestation of the power of the owning class. While these phenomenally rich individuals and corporations can give their money to positive social projects, they can decide to take it away as well, or do something radically different with it, or just stuff it away and not invest in anything. The choice is theirs and by making choices with such huge consequences over millions of people, they exercise *power*, which again is traditionally seen to be the enemy of freedom, as reviewed in the Introduction. After all, if positive works are all that's required to justify power, it's easy to point to history's many generous kings and "benevolent dictators." Are these figures justified in having power, since they sometimes cared to use it for generous purposes? Or is this still an unfree social configuration, since these societies were still one dictator's stroke or royal mood swing away from having these nice projects taken away and replaced by horrible enterprises?

An example of the whims of today's great philanthropic foundations came from Michael Bloomberg, former mayor of New York and worth an estimated $48 billion, when he said to the press casually, "I'd argue another gift to fight a disease that has a lot of the world's attention and people are focusing on it is not where I want us to go."[130] Or as a *Forbes* headline put it, Bloomberg is "Bored With Philanthropy."[131] So if the current epidemic is getting dull and played out, you, the billionaire, can yawn and pass on funding it, and put your foundation money toward a new, more cutting-edge cause to talk about at elite parties.

A final crucial problem is that in this era of tax cuts for wealthy households and resulting government budget deficits, many advocates of cutting government services or the social safety net point to private philanthropy and "faith-based" organizations as being able to step into their place. But this is immediately ludicrous—private charities, even on the scale reviewed here, are nowhere near able to pay independently for a country's total social needs—from housing the insane to providing vaccines.

The foundations themselves recognize this, as when Patty Stonesifer, then chief of the Gates Foundation, said "Our giving is a drop in the bucket compared to the government's responsibility."[132] This was confirmed recently, when the Foundation committed $50 million to fight the current Ebola outbreak in West Africa. In contrast, the UN estimates the total cost of containing the outbreak at roughly $600 million.[133]

Definitely within the reach of these modern foundations, but far from the kind of reliable commitment they are known to make. Friedman himself acknowledges this issue when he says in *Capitalism and Freedom,* "Freedom is a tenable objective only for responsible individuals. We do not believe in freedom for madmen or children... It would be nice if we could rely on voluntary activities of individuals to house and care for the madmen. But I think we cannot rule out the possibility that such charitable activities will be inadequate,"[134] so even leading "libertarians" may concede that there are limits to ruling-class munificence.

Also, it has to be recognized that quite commonly, philanthropy is a costly but very valuable way to clean up your plutocratic image. Business historians observe that Rockefeller felt a religious drive for his donations, but they see, too, that "Philanthropy also held an earthly reward for Rockefeller: It helped transform his legacy from that of a predatory monopolist to one of the most generous donors of his century."[135] This commercial ulterior motive also applies to more modern philanthropic giants like the Gates Foundation, where the business press reviews the intriguing history of its origin: "Twenty years ago, people associated the name Gates with 'ruthless, predatory' monopolistic conduct," and quoting a wealth adviser: "His philanthropy has helped 'rebrand' his name." The power of charity is simple: "after taking a public relations beating during [the Microsoft antitrust] trial's early going in late 1998, the company started what was described at the time as a 'charm offensive' aimed at improving its image... Mr. Gates contributed $20.3 billion, or 71 percent of his total contributions to the foundation... during the 18 months between the start of the trial and the verdict."[136]

Or consider the donors to the Clinton Foundation, "a who's who of some of the world's wealthiest people," as *The Wall Street Journal* called it, years before it became an election issue.[137] The donor list showed that the Foundation is funded by powerful elites who are not exactly champions of freedom, including the Monarchy of the Kingdom of Saudi Arabia, Ukrainian steel "oligarchs" and Blackwater, the US mercenary company under legal sanction for its killings in Iraq.[138] Big Charity remains a ruling-class pastime.

Meanwhile, the average American's recreation, like taking in the ball game on TV, has remained an ad-traffic plaything of the great US corporate oligopolies. The traditional first pitch of a baseball game used to be an occasional ceremony with a public figure. Today, the tradition is a component of large commercial contracts between the team franchise and sponsors, "regarded as a marketing opportunity, a sweetener in sponsorship deals between baseball teams and groups that want a piece of the spotlight," as the business press reports.[139] "Sometimes, there are ceremonial second, third, and fourth and fifth pitches." The admirable figures honored by a pitch in front of a regional commercial market include representatives of banks, media networks and "reality" TV shows.

Of course, these class-driven lifestyles do have devoted defenders, like Hayek and the Friedmans. If they don't speak up for the rich and powerful, who will?

Ups and Downs and Downs

Having reviewed power in the market, the resulting class lifestyles and the fig leaf of philanthropy, we should take up the issue of stability and freedom. The regular need for basic goods among living people means that economic downturns or financial crises put employers in stronger positions of power relative to their workforce. And with the US and world economies now in an ongoing, volatile semi-depression along class lines, it illustrates that some basic stability, or security, is needed for real freedom. Hayek specially addresses this in a chapter of *The Road to*

Serfdom called "Security and Freedom" and he recognizes "the supremely important problem of combating general fluctuations in economic activity and the recurrent waves of large-scale unemployment which accompany them. This is, of course, one of the gravest and most pressing problems of our time."[140] These fluctuations are called the "business cycle" — an irregular but persistent pattern of ups and downs in market activity. Employment tends to follow this pattern, meaning that when the market shrinks, or enters "recession," there is a very consistent decrease in the number of jobs.

But Hayek's weak-sauce ideology implies that while wild swings of fortune and the resulting suffering "offends our sense of justice… in the world as it is men are, in fact, not likely to give their best for long periods unless their own interests are directly involved. At least for great numbers some external pressure is needed if they are to give their best."[141] Hayek's elitism is fairly open and will come up again in Chapter 2.

This same reactionary view is expressed in a broader frame by early Austrian economist Joseph Schumpeter, famous in the field for his concept of "creative destruction," in which markets are continuously changing, creating new goods and ways of doing business, and simultaneously destroying the value of previous goods or ways of producing them. As he wrote in his most prominent work, *Capitalism, Socialism and Democracy*, "The essential point to grasp is that in dealing with capitalism we are dealing with an evolutionary process… Capitalism, then, is by nature a form or method of economic change and not only never is but never can be stationary."[142] But an economy that "never can be stationary" can also never be stable or secure, as far as an individual or family in it is concerned. In a system engaged in constant churn, there can be little confidence that a career will not be destroyed. And the workforce of the twenty-first century knows all too well that it is considered totally disposable when change happens.

A common wrongheaded opinion related to this issue is that the unemployed are lazy and could surely find work if they would try harder, like when US right-wing icon Glenn Beck said of workers drawing long-term unemployment in the stagnant post-2008 depression, "I bet you'd be ashamed to call them Americans."[143] Apparently reactionary boobs like Beck believe that literally millions of working people are suddenly simultaneously struck by a contagious case of being a shiftless jerk right at the beginning of a recession.

The power dynamic caused by the business cycle is similar to that caused by "capital mobility," the freedom of businesses to move their capital and production around the world, compared to the limited "labor mobility." One of the great accounts of modern capital mobility is *Capital Moves*, Jefferson Cowie's book about RCA, the electronics firm. "Each of RCA's plant relocations represents the corporation's response to workers' increasing sense of entitlement and control over investment in their community. Capital flight was a means of countering that control as the company sought out new reservoirs of controllable labor." But "In each location, a glut of potential employees shrank over time into a tightening labor market, once-deferential workers organized into a union shop, and years of toil on the shop floor recast docility into a contentious and demanding, if isolated and ambivalent, working class. The geographic terrain inhabited by capital was far larger than labor's niche, however," with RCA moving first to the US South and then internationally.[144]

By now, stories are everywhere of this capital mobility and the wrenching instability it means for the workforce, leaving communities and whole regions behind. And as anyone knows who has lived in a town after it loses a major employer, the ripple effects are serious—the laid-off workers no longer have the money to spend, so local businesses see a big drop in business, so they in turn lay off staff, which aggravates the situation. Soon, the town may be ruined economically or even turned into a ghost town. This is the power of capital investment, in one of its modern forms—the ability to remove or create capital assets and an employment base, according to shifting strategies.

Maybe the definitive instance of capital mobility today is the former citadel of American industrial strength, Detroit. Once the great center of US manufacturing, and in fact the core of the productive juggernaut that won the World Wars and awed the world with wealth production, Detroit in 2014 was history's largest municipal bankruptcy. And the fundamental reason was accurately fingered by *The Wall Street Journal*: "years of capital flight."[145]

Compare this mobility of capital with the mobility of people after a job loss. Yale economist Charles Lindbolm:

> People must move, leave their homes, change their occupations—any of a number of possible major changes, none of their own choosing... A person whose style of life and family livelihood have for years been built around a particular job, occupation or location finds a command backed by a threat to fire him indistinguishable in many consequences for his liberty from a command backed by the police and the courts... Income-earning property is a bulwark only for those who have it![146]

And without it, each of us is subject to the shifting winds of private investment, which may move our work across many international borders, with us unfree to follow even if we wanted. And today's refugee crisis makes efforts to leave your home country look especially unattractive. The desperate global reality of "labor mobility" includes the nightmarish Mediterranean "ghost ships" crammed with Syrian, Iraqi, Afghan, and African immigrants and literally pointed at Greece or Italy and set on autopilot.[147] Or the extremely dangerous "death train" ride on freight rails across Mexico by penniless Central American migrants, hoping to reach the US or Canada.

It's also essential to observe that recessions are more severe following a financial crisis, clearly proven by the wave of major crashes since the deregulation of finance in the "neoliberal" policy era of the Age of Friedman. Harvard economists Carmen Reinhart and Kenneth Rogoff document that giant financial crises, like those common today, typically follow financial deregulation. Their extensive review concludes that *"Periods of high international capital mobility have repeatedly produced international banking crises, not only famously, as they did in the 1990s, but historically."*[148]

Recessions started by financial crashes also usually involve heavy amounts of debt, used to make large purchases during good times, like a house, a car, or building a business. Recently, people in the professional and working classes have been more likely to go into debt just to cover basic expenses, since their incomes have been flat or shrinking for forty years. This huge growth in debt, from mortgages in the housing crisis to student loans for young people hoping to help their odds, creates an enormous burden for the regular classes when the business cycle lurches into recession or worse. Today's personal debt levels are awful to contemplate, especially in the US, where the country's trillion dollars in credit card debt was only recently eclipsed by over a trillion dollars in student loan debt.[149] This debt represents significant power by creditors over their borrowers—reflecting class power.

A hilarious example of this is the recent growth in "starter interrupt" devices, installed in cars sold to high-risk "subprime" borrowers, typically those with low or stretched middle-class incomes. These devices disable cars if the recipient of the loan goes into default or sometimes after merely missing a payment. Present in millions of cars and trucks, these allow "lenders to retain the ultimate control," as *The New York Times* describes.[150] The lenders' devices can make cars "shut down while idling at stoplights" and also feature "tracking capabilities that allow lenders and others to know the movements of borrowers... And the warnings the devices emit—beeps that become more persistent as the due date for the loan payment approaches—are seen by some borrowers as more degrading than helpful." Yet Hayek wrote, "What is called economic power, while it can be an instrument of coercion, is, in the hands of private individuals, never exclusive or complete power, never power over the whole life of a person."[151] One wonders.

All these factors—the business cycle, heightened capital concentration and mobility, union decline, the growth of debt and the return of serial financial crisis—point to a drastic reduction in the security and certainly the bargaining position of the workforce. And in fact that's the view of at least one prominent right-wing economist—Alan Greenspan, the former Chair of the Federal Reserve and longtime Ayn Rand fan. Speaking in the late 1990s, Greenspan attempted to account for why the relatively tight job markets of the time were failing to translate into growth in wages. "Because workers are more worried about their own job security and their marketability if forced to change jobs, they are apparently accepting smaller increases in their compensation at any given level of labor-market tightness," he said.[152] Thus, the conservative *Wall Street Journal* found in 2011 that since the 2008 crash, "companies shared only 6% of productivity gains with their workers."[153] Today's workforce, according to the Age of Friedman's own supporters, runs on fear.

In the face of all this, Hayek says that any measures to ensure worker security must be strictly limited, even if the result hurts: "It is essential that we should relearn frankly to face the fact that freedom can be had only at a price and that as individuals we must be prepared to make severe material sacrifices to preserve our liberty."[154] Freedom, indeed. The power wielded by capital and its threats to move is a quite decisive violation of negative freedom.

Perhaps most damningly of all, we can consider the testimony of Frederick Douglass, escaped slave and public intellectual:

> As the laborer becomes more intelligent he will develop what capital he already possesses—that is the power to organize and combine for its own protection. Experience demonstrates that there may be a slavery of wages only a little less galling and crushing in its effects than chattel slavery, and that this slavery of wages must go down with the other... those who would reproach us should remember that it is hard for labor, however fortunately and favorably surrounded, to cope with the tremendous power of capital in any contest for higher wages or improved condition... The man who has it in his power to say to a man, you must work the land for me for such wages as I choose to give, has a power of slavery over him as real, if not as complete, as he who compels toil under the lash. All that a man hath he will give for his life.[155]

Unlike Douglass, Friedman and Hayek side with the power of "the fortunate ones of the earth," King's "reactionaries" and "despots," and Smith's "masters." They pay no attention to the oligopolies owned by Citigroup's "plutonomy" and "1 percent," and their "The public be damned" island-buying arrogance. Their weak-sauce ideology focuses instead on those shady "defensive combinations of the workmen" and the "charm offensive" philanthropy of the rich. Humanity works for a worldwide ruling-class rogue's gallery dressed by obedient intellectuals as freedom. The open hand giveth, and the invisible hand taketh away.

Endnotes

1.   Adam Smith, *The Wealth of Nations*, Indianapolis, IN: Liberty*Classics*, 1981, p. 84, 83.

2. Frederick Douglass in Philip Foner and Yvonne Taylor, eds, *Frederick Douglass: Selected Speeches and Writings*, Chicago, IL: Chicago Review Press, 1999, p. 676, 678.

3. Gallup, "Americans Less Satisfied With Freedom," 1 July 2014.

4. GlobeScan, "One-in-Two Say Internet Unsafe Place for Expressing Views: Global Poll," BBC World Service, 31 March 2014.

5. Nick Hanauer, "The Pitchforks Are Coming...For Us Plutocrats," *Politico Magazine*, July/August 2014.

6. Manuel Klausner, "Inside Ronald Reagan," *Reason*, July 1975.

7. Ronald Reagan, "Free to Choose," https://www.youtube.com/watch?v=um-p3ZhiO60.

8. Rush Limbaugh, "Milton Friedman Schools Phil Donahue (and Barack Obama) on Capitalism and Greed", 31 July 2012.

9. William Buckley, "Milton Friedman, R.I.P." *National Review*, Vol. 58, No. 23, 18 December 2006.

10. Milton Friedman, "Freedom's Friend," *Wall Street Journal*, 11 June 2004.

11. Stephen Moore, "All Friedmanites now," *National Review*, Vol. 50, No. 14, 3 August 1998.

12. Milton Friedman, *Capitalism and Freedom*, Chicago, IL: University of Chicago Press, 2002, p. 8–9.

13. Milton and Rose Friedman, *Free to Choose*, New York: Harcourt, 1990, p. 222–3.

14. Justin LaHart, "The Glenn Beck Effect: Hayek Has a Hit," Real Time Economics (*The Wall Street Journal*), 17 June 2010.

15. Friedrich Hayek, *The Road to Serfdom*, Chicago: University of Chicago Press, 2007, p. 69, 67.

16. *Ibid*, p. 86.

17. Murray Rothbard, *Man, Economy and State with Power and Market*, Auburn, AL: Ludwig von Mises Institute, 2009, p.

515.

18. *Ibid*, p. 20, p. 14.

19. Friedman, *Capitalism and Freedom*, p. 163–4.

20. Ludwig von Mises, *Human Action*, Auburn, AL: The Ludwig von Mises Institute, 1998, p. 138–9.

21. Jennifer Burns, *Goddess of the Market*, New York: Oxford University Press, 2009, p. 177; cited in Corey Robin, *The Reactionary Mind*, New York: Oxford University Press, 2011, p. 91.

22. Priscilla Murolo and A.B. Chitty, *From the Folks Who Brought You the Weekend*, New York: The New Press, 2001, p. 120.

23. Friedman, *Capitalism and Freedom*, p.15.

24. Charles Koch, "I'm Fighting to Restore a Free Society," *Wall Street Journal*, 2 April 2014.

25. Friedmans, *Free to Choose*, p. 136.

26. *Ibid*, p. 135.

27. Rothbard, *Man, Economy, and State with Power and Market*, p. 656.

28. Hayek, *The Road to Serfdom*, p. 135–6.

29. Friedman, *Capitalism and Freedom*, p. 168.

30. Mises, *Human Action*, p. 803.

31. Matthew Josephson, *The Robber Barons*, New York: Houghton Mifflin, 1934, p. 414–5.

32. Thomas Piketty, *Capital in the Twenty-First Century*, Cambridge, MA: Belknap Press, 2014, p. 349.

33. *Ibid*, p. 344; Joachim Frick and Markus Grabka, "Wealth Inequality On the Rise In Germany," German Institute For Economic Research, 28 May 2009; Christina Larson, "China's 1 Percent vs. America's 1 Percent," *Bloomberg Businessweek*, 28 July 2014.

34. Piketty, p. 438.

35. *Ibid*, p. 257, 259.

36. *Ibid*, p. 260.

37. Lawrence Mishel, *et al*, *The State of Working America*, 12th ed.

Ithaca, NY: Cornell University Press, 2012, p. 387.

38. Ajay Kapur, *et al*, "Plutonomy: Buying Luxury, Explaining Global Imbalances," Citigroup, 16 October 2005; Ajay Kapur, *et al*, "The Global Investigator: The Plutonomy Symposium—Rising Tides Lifting Yachts," Citigroup, 29 September 2006.

39. Myles Udland, "Bank of America Merrill Lynch Is 'Comfortable With the Thrust' Of Piketty's Analysis," *Business Insider*, 30 May 2014.

40. Nelson Schwartz, "The Middle Class Is Steadily Eroding. Just Ask the Business World," *New York Times*, 2 February 2014.

41. Katie Quan in Michael Zweig, ed, *What's Class Got To Do With It?*, Ithaca, NY: Cornell University Press, 2004, p. 95.

42. Barbara Ehrenreich, *Fear of Falling*, New York: Pantheon, 1989, p. 15.

43. Friedman, *Capitalism and Freedom*, p. 23.

44. Robin Hahnel, *The ABCs of Political Economy*, London: Pluto Press, 2014, p. 273.

45. Amartya Sen, *Poverty and Famines*, London: Oxford, 1990, p. 1.

46. Russell Baker, "Observer: Legally, Rich Is Best," *New York Times*, 27 May 1969.

47. Friedmans, *Free to Choose*, p. 222–3.

48. Friedman, *Capitalism and Freedom*, p. 120.

49. Mises, *Human Action*, p. 359.

50. Friedman, *Capitalism and Freedom*, p. 15–6.

51. *Ibid*, p. 121.

52. Paul Krugman and Robin Wells, *Microeconomics*, 3rd ed. New York: Worth, 2013, p. 425.

53. Barry Lynn, *Cornered*, Hoboken, NJ: John Wiley & Sons, 2010, p. 6.

54. *Ibid*, p. 32.

55. *Ibid*, p. 38.

56. Tripp Mickle and Saabira Chaudhuri, "AB InBev's SABMiller Deal Still Faces Hurdles," *Wall Street Journal*, 11 November 2015.

57. *Ibid*, p. 91–2.

58. Hayek, *The Road to Serfdom*, p. 91.

59. Wilford Eiteman and Glen Guthrie, "The Shape of the Average Cost Curve," *American Economic Review*, Vol. 42, December 1952.

60. Alfred Chandler, *Scale and Scope*, Cambridge, MA: Harvard University Press, 1994, p. 23–4, 26.

61. *Ibid*, p. 76.

62. Douglas Dowd, *Inequality and the Global Economic Crisis*, London: Pluto Press, 2009, p. 62.

63. Steve Keen, *Debunking Economics*, London: Pluto Press, 2001, p. 104-5.

64. Pankaj Ghemawat, "Sustainable Advantage," *Harvard Business Review*, Vol. 64, No. 5, September-October 1986.

65. Charles Fishman, *The Wal-Mart Effect*, New York: Penguin, 2007, p. 95, 79.

66. Barry Lynn, "Breaking the Chain," *Harper's Magazine*, July 2006.

67. Paul Constant, "It's Time to Turn Your Back on Amazon," *The Stranger*, 30 May 2014.

68. Brad Stone, *The Everything Store*, New York: Little, Brown and Company, 2013, p. 243–4.

69. *Ibid*, p. 245.

70. Greg Bensinger, "An Amazon-Disney Dispute Erupts," *The Wall Street Journal*, 11 August 2014.

71. Leslie Kaufman, "Hachette Adds Heft to Combat Amazon," *The New York Times*, 24 June 2014.

72. Lynn, *Cornered*, 2010, p. 54.

73. Amy Martinez and Kristi Heim, "Amazon a virtual no-show in hometown philanthropy," *The Seattle Times*, 31 March 2012.

74. Friedman, *Capitalism and Freedom*, p. 29.
75. Mina Kimes, "Railroads: Cartel or Free Market Success Story?" *Fortune*, 13 September 2011.
76. Friedman, *Capitalism and Freedom*, p. 28.
77. *Ibid*, p. 128.
78. Don Clark and Robert McMillan, "Giants Tighten Grip on Internet Economy,"*The Wall Street Journal*, November 6 2015.
79. Tim Wu, *The Master Switch*, New York: Vintage, 2011, p. 280.
80. Farhad Manjoo, "Tech's 'Frightful 5' Will Dominate Digital Life for Foreseeable Future,"*The New York Times*, January 20, 2016.
81. Lynn, *Cornered*, p. 117.
82. Edward Herman, "A Brief History of Mergers and Antitrust Policy," *Dollars & Sense*, May/June 1998.
83. Leonard Silk, "Antitrust Issues Facing Reagan,"*The New York Times*, 13 February 1981.
84. Steven Pearlstein, "Arguments for Whirlpool-Maytag Just Don't Wash,"*The Washington Post*, 22 February 2006.
85. Chandler, *The Visible Hand*, p. 375.
86. Friedmans, *Free to Choose*, p. 225.
87. Anthony Bianco, "Exxon Unleashed," *Businessweek,* 8 April 2001.
88. US Census Bureau, *American FactFinder*, Establishments/ Firms, Concentration of Firms, "Manufacturing: Subject Series" and "Information: Subject Series," retrieved 19 August 2016.
89. Josephson, *The Robber Barons*, p. 15.
90. Rothbard, p. 654.
91. George Orwell, *As I Please*, New York: Nonpareil, 2000, p.118.
92. Friedmans, *Free to Choose*, p. 246.
93. *Ibid*, p.245.
94. Friedman, *Capitalism and Freedom*, p. 13.

95. Richard Freeman, "Do Workers Still Want Unions? *More Than Ever*," EPI Briefing Paper #102, 22 February 2007; Aaron Bernstein, "Can This Man Save Labor?" *Businessweek*, 13 September 2004.

96. Lydia Saad, "Americans' Support for Labor Unions Continues to Recover," Gallup, 17 August 2015.

97. Martin Luther King, Jr., in Michael Honey, ed., *"All Labor Has Dignity,"* Boston: Beacon Press, 2011, p. 113, 90.

98. *Ibid*, p. 36, 38.

99. *Ibid*, p. 17, 177.

100. *Ibid*, p. 22.

101. Mishel *et al*, *The State of Working America*, p. 269.

102. Roger Martin, "In America, Labor Is Friendless," *Harvard Business Review* blog, 28 August 2014.

103. Aaron Bernstein, "Can This Man Save Labor?" *Businessweek*, 13 September 2004.

104. Friedmans, *Free to Choose*, p. 235-6.

105. Robert Brady, *Business As a System of Power*, New York: Columbia University Press, 1943, p. 195.

106. *Ibid*, p. 213, 201.

107. Hayek, *The Road to Serfdom*, p. 165.

108. Brady, *Business As a System of Power*, p. 210.

109. Smith, *The Wealth of Nations*, p. 83–5.

110. Hayek, *The Road to Serfdom*, p. 205.

111. *Ibid*, p. 204.

112. Murolo and Chitty, *From the Folks Who Brought You the Weekend*, p. 111.

113. Mark Ames, Techtopus, "How Silicon Valley's most celebrated CEOs conspired to drive down 100,000 tech engineers' wages," 23 January 2014.

114. James Stewart, "Steve Jobs, a Genius at Pushing Boundaries,"*The New York Times*, 2 May 2014.

115. Jeff Elder, "Tech Giants Discussed Hiring, Say Documents, *"The Wall Street Journal*, 21 April 2014.

116. Dean Baker, "Silicon Valley billionaires believe in the free market, as long as they benefit," *The Guardian*, 3 February 2014.

117. Mishel *et al*, *The State of Working America*, 12th ed 397–8.

118. Robin Finn, "New York's Once and Future Mansions,"*The New York Times*, 5 September 2014.

119. Michelle Higgins, "For the New York Condo Owner With Everything, a Million-Dollar Parking Spot,"*The New York Times*, 9 September 2014.

120. Ginia Bellafante, "On the Upper West Side, a House Divided by Income,"*The New York Times*, 25 July 2014.

121. Hilary Osborne, "Poor doors: the segregation of London's inner-city flat dwellers," *The Guardian*, 25 July 2014.

122. Adam Lusher, "Were 'Poor Doors' added to mixed developments so wealthy residents don't have to go in alongside social housing tenants?" *The Independent*, 25 July 2014.

123. Elizabeth Harris, "Why Buy a Condo You Seldom Use? Because You Can,"*The New York Times*, 11 February 2013.

124. Sara Clemence, "Hotels Race to Create the Best Suites,"*The Wall Street Journal*, 23 August 2013.

125. Julian Guthrie, "Larry Ellison's Fantasy Island,"*The Wall Street Journal*, 13 June 2013.

126. Peter Bernstein and Annalyn Swan, *All the Money in the World*, New York: Knopf, 2007, p. 208–9.

127. Milton and Rose Friedman, *Free to Choose*, New York: Harcourt, 1990, p. 36.

128. *Ibid*, p. 139.

129. Bernstein and Swan, *All the Money in the World*, p.280.

130. Paul Sullivan, "Private Citizen Bloomberg's Philosophy on Philanthropy,"*The New York Times*, 25 April 2014.

131. Agustino Fontevecchia, "Bored of Philanthropy, Billionaire Mike Bloomberg Back As Chief At Bloomberg LP," *Forbes*, 3 September 2014.

132. Bernstein and Swan, *All the Money in the World*, p. 279.

133. Donald McNeil, "Gates Foundation Pledges $50 Million to Fight Ebola," *The New York Times*, 10 September 2014.

134. Friedman, *Capitalism and Freedom*, p. 33.

135. Bernstein and Swan, *All the Money in the World*, p. 280.

136. Randall Smith, "As His Foundation Has Grown, Gates Has Slowed His Donations," *The New York Times*, 26 May 2014.

137. Susan Schmidt, Margaret Coker and Jay Solomon, "Clinton Reveals Donors—Charity Got $140 Million Abroad," *The Wall Street Journal*, 19 December 2008.

138. Rachel Zoll, "Saudis, Indians Among Clinton Foundation Donors," Associated Press, 18 December 2008.

139. Andrew Keh, "Tonight's Honored Guest on the Mound, a Backflipping Frog," *The New York Times*, 28 May 2013.

140. Hayek, *The Road to Serfdom*, p. 148–9.

141. *Ibid*, p. 149-50, 151.

142. Joseph Schumpeter, *Capitalism, Socialism, and Democracy*, London: Routledge, 2003, p. 82.

143. Glenn Beck, *Glenn Beck*, 16 August 2014, http://mediamatters. org/video/2010/08/16/beck-on-some-99er-protesters-i-betyoud-be-asha/169275.

144. Jefferson Cowie, *Capital Moves*, New York: The New Press, 1999, p. 4.

145. Douglas Lavin, "Michigan's boom brings better times to cities blighted by unemployment," *The Wall Street Journal*, 25 January 1995.

146. Charles Lindblom, *Politics and Markets*, New York: Basic Books, 1977, p. 48–50.

147. Giada Zampano and Matina Stevis, "'Ghost Ships' Leave Refugees Adrift," *The Wall Street Journal*, 2 January 2015.

148. Carmen Reinhart and Kenneth Rogoff, *This Time Is Different*, Princeton, NJ: Princeton University Press, 2009, p. 155-6.

149. Susanne Soederberg, "The Student Loan Crisis and the Debtfare State," *Dollars & Sense*, May/June 2015.

150. Michael Corkery and Jessica Silver-Greenberg, "Miss a Payment? Good Luck Moving That Car,"*The New York Times*, 24 September 2014.

151. *Ibid*, p. 166.

152. David Wessel, "Fed Chief Sets Monetary Policy By Seat-of the-Pants Approach,"*The Wall Street Journal*, 27 January 1997.

153. Mark Whitehouse, "Workers Not Benefiting From Productivity Gains,"*The Wall Street Journal*, 5 March 2011.

154. Hayek, *The Road to Serfdom*, p. 156.

155. Frederick Douglass in Philip Foner and Yuval Taylor, eds, *Frederick Douglass: Selected Speeches and Writings*, Chicago, IL: Chicago Review Press, 1999, p. 676–8.

Chapter 2

Pennies For Your Thoughts
Freedom of Information

Under existing conditions, private capitalists inevitably control, directly or indirectly, the main sources of information (press, radio, education). It is thus extremely difficult, and indeed, in most cases quite impossible, for the individual citizen to come to objective conclusions and to make intelligent use of his political rights.
Albert Einstein[1]

The twentieth century has been characterized by three developments of great political importance: the growth of democracy, the growth of corporate power, and the growth of corporate propaganda as a means of protecting corporate power against democracy.
Alex Carey[2]

Among our different freedoms, the liberty to share information and learn about the world is among the most important. To the man on the street, attempts to control the flow of information quickly attract suspicion and opposition. We normally associate heavy restrictions on information with dictatorships, along with propaganda—the manipulative use of repetitive, one-sided information. John Stuart Mill wrote in his seminal *On Liberty* that attempts "to control the expression of opinion" are intolerable, even if the institution responsible represents the public will: "The power itself is illegitimate."[3] A common conservative view of this subject holds that such attempts generally originate in government, while on the other hand the market "turns out to be a more efficient mechanism for digesting dispersed information than any that man has deliberately designed,"[4] as Friedrich Hayek put it.

But the market economy has a long tradition of information control, too; for example in the work of Edward Bernays, who's considered to be the central founder of modern public relations and who helped organize the government Creel Committee to encourage public support for World War I. He went on to spend most of his career working for private sector giants—Alcoa, Proctor & Gamble, Lucky Strike cigarettes—and as he put it, the inventors of the new field of propaganda "applied (on behalf of business) the publicity methods they had learned in the war." Bernays found in his work that even in market economies, "We are governed, our minds molded, our tastes formed, our ideas suggested, largely by men we have never heard of."[5]

This practice is very important in the real-world marketplace of gigantic firms, concentrated markets and sharply skewed wealth that was described in Chapter 1. The exercise of market power takes its own form in the information and media markets, and with a special importance: control over knowledge is a major barrier to any fundamental social change that could address these structural problems we're dealing with. It turns out that with a free market of information, you're free to be patronized by the billionaire media property of your choice.

The Price is Righteous

The traditional conservative picture has been that free markets allow for a free flow of information. As described in Chapter 1, Hayek saw most government action as the first step on the "Road to Serfdom," ending inevitably in the gross dictatorships that were emerging as he wrote in Nazi Austria. Totalitarian governments, he correctly observed, tend to control information until:

The word 'truth' itself ceases to have its old meaning. It describes no longer something to be found, with the individual conscience as the sole arbiter... it becomes something to be laid down by authority... The general intellectual climate which this produces, the spirit of complete cynicism as regards truth which it engenders, the loss of the sense of even the meaning of truth... the way in which differences of opinion in every branch of knowledge become political issues to be decided by authority, are all things which one must personally experience — no short description can convey their extent.[6]

Hayek was far less concerned about a handful of separate centers of information control rather than just one, as we'll see.

Building on this traditional belief in the general freedom of information in markets, economists often focus on the systematic way markets provide specifically economic information, which is through *prices*. Prices from this perspective are essentially pieces of information about how relatively scarce different goods are, in terms of the resources needed to make them — how many resources are required to make a book compared to a bulldozer, for example. The theory goes that any change in the conditions of a market, like a change in consumer diet preferences, will be transmitted automatically through a free market because of changes in the price of some foods relative to others.

Glenn Hubbard, of the conservative American Enterprise Institute and the main designer of the 2003 Bush administration's tax cuts, summarized this "market mechanism" that relies on free-flowing information:

Changes in *relative prices* — that is, the price of one good or service relative to other goods or services — provides information, or a signal, to both consumers and firms. For example, in 2010, consumers world-wide increased their demand for cattle and poultry. Because corn is fed to cattle and poultry, prices for corn soared relative to prices for other crops. Many farmers in the United States received this price signal and responded by increasing the amount of corn they planted.[7]

This simple concept of market prices is held up by the economics profession and the Right as a special merit of market economies—their ability to quickly transmit huge amounts of information as easily understood price movements. The Friedmans wrote about how price signals adjust economic production around the world:

> No one sitting in a central office gave orders to these thousands of people... The price system is the mechanism that performs this task without central direction, without requiring people to speak to one another or to like one another... People who can use the information have an incentive to get it and they are in a position to do so.[8]

Crucially, this picture of the free transmission of market information is based on an expectation of "competitive" markets with many diverse firms, as discussed in Chapter 1. The importance of competition for an information market is that if a company provides incorrect or misleading information, companies or investors paying for that information will discover it's poor and turn elsewhere. Having somewhere else to turn implies other firms and, indeed, a large number of them. So a competitive aspect of markets is crucial here just as it was in the more general cases in the last chapter. But as we've seen, to economists as long as a market is "free," meaning free of government meddling, it is simply assumed to be diverse and competitive.

Hayek took this abstract picture of prices to the next level. He wrote in the prestigious *American Economic Review* that

"The peculiar character of the problem of a rational economic order is determined precisely by the fact that the knowledge of the circumstances of which we must make use never exists in concentrated or integrated form, but solely as the dispersed bits of incomplete and frequently contradictory knowledge which all the separate individuals possess."[9] In other words, modern economies are hugely complex with millions of different people and companies making billions of decisions, so the only way to deal with that much complex data is to let the market aggregate a price through supply and demand. Without anyone having to try a comprehensive calculation, markets automatically organize the information.

For this reason, Hayek concluded that "It is more than metaphor to describe the price system as a kind of machinery for registering change, or a system of telecommunications which enables individual producers to watch merely the movement of a few points," but he went further and seemed to grant divine, godlike stature to the market's pricing system. "I am convinced that if it were the result of deliberate human design... this mechanism would have been acclaimed as one of the greatest triumphs of the human mind. Its misfortune is the double one that it is not the product of human design and that the people guided by it usually do not know why they are made to do what they do."

This leaves the Right's picture of market information pretty clear—markets transmit information automatically, without conscious human choice, and summarize huge amounts of data into simple changes in prices or other data. They allow for many diverse sources of information. They organize our lives. They wield the shining sword of truth. Hallelujah!

The Press Compressed

These over-the-top fantasies can only be sustained through a level of abstraction that leaves out several problems with this rosy picture of market information, some of which will come up separately in Chapter 4. The biggest problems with these views come from the question of power reviewed in Chapter 1: markets consolidate over time, firms grow large and gain cost advantages and then market power, and the wealthy owners of the small numbers of gigantic companies share a class interest that guides their decision-making. That class interest is exemplified by the literally total absence of labor leaders from US Sunday news talk shows in the first two-thirds of 2014, while CEOs and pro-business analysts dominated.[10]

In fact, these uniquely important markets involving information and communication actually have an especially strong tendency to consolidate and form oligopolies themselves, unless some public regulation limits that somewhat. This tendency is an example of "network effects." Markets that require a network of some type for their use, like air travel or telephone service, become more valuable to consumers as more consumers use them. When more airports open, the local airport gains new value for consumers since they can fly to more destinations. Much the same has always been true of communications and media markets.

The hard numbers are recorded in the US Economic Census, which gathers information including the level of concentration in different markets; although it bears repeating that these official stats understate the issue. Still, the 2007 results, the most recent available, are pretty impressive. The four largest cable providers in total reached 68.3 percent of the total market, the eight largest Internet service providers served 48.7 percent of the market, the eight largest newspaper publishers earned 44.9 percent of market income, the eight largest radio networks were heard by 73.7 percent of the audience and the four largest Web search portals were used by a whopping 90.6 percent of the market.[11] Even these understated levels of concentration numbers are completely divorced from the picture casually implied by Friedman and Hayek above.

These high media-consolidation levels did not exist until relatively recently, where the pattern of market evolution seen in Chapter 1 appears again, most recently helped by the relaxing of antitrust limits to concentration and the deregulatory Telecommunications Act of 1996. The Act removed many media ownership caps (limits to how many media outlets one firm or individual can own) and also allowed cable, phone and media companies to compete in delivering data to households. The idea was, according to the Congressional summary, "to provide for a pro-competitive, de-regulatory national policy framework" for communication.[12] One major component was "wire-to-wire competition," the removal of limitations on media cross-ownership, allowing media firms to merge into different branches of the market—so the phone companies could buy cable companies, media conglomerates could buy cable networks to accompany their cable channels and so on.

But media merger coverage in the anti-regulation *Wall Street Journal* still reported the common pattern of deregulation and consolidation often seen in the rest of the economy. Following the Act, a *Journal* headline described one of the many resulting enormous mergers, between Comcast and AT&T Broadband, which "Cements the Rise of an Oligopoly In the Cable Business."[13] It reported, "After the phone and cable industries were thrown open to competition in 1996" the FCC and industry "predicted a boom for consumers." But instead, the deregulation started "a new phase in the hyper-consolidation of the cable industry... An industry that was once a hodgepodge of family-owned companies has become one of the nation's most visible and profitable oligopolies, as smaller operators are unable to cope with the rising costs of the business." And it's not just the *Journal's* opinion—an NBC ex-exec is quoted actually saying "The big media companies are quietly re-creating the 'old programming oligopoly' of the pre-cable era" as the largest top-tier media firms now reach over 80 percent of the prime-time TV audience, through their subsidiaries and parent networks.[14]

So the expectations of "free" market advocates have failed another test—rather than becoming a rich, free, diverse market environment after deregulation reduced the coercive hand of the government, the industry became more consolidated and less diverse. If people have any "positive freedom" to multiple sources of news and entertainment, free markets frequently work against that. The conservative *Journal* itself notes the common features of network-based industries:

The cable mating dance mirrors a similar frenzy long under way in the phone industry, leaving the nation's two essential communications lines in the hands of powerful oligopolies. It's a scenario also unfolding for the nation's airlines, another industry where deregulation set off a flurry of mergers, creating a short roster of powerful giants. And consumers are, in many cases, paying the price.[15]

This conservative business reporting tracks closely with the conclusions of radical media analysts like Robert McChesney, Professor of Communication at the University of Illinois at Urbana-Champaign, who lays out the issue of media market structure in the most fundamental terms, describing:

Vast conglomerates that function as oligopolies in not just one media market but in many. In media, as elsewhere, these monopolistic/oligopolistic markets are predicated upon high barriers to entry that severely limit the ability of small start-up media firms to enter the market successfully... Firms in oligopolistic markets have much greater leverage over their suppliers (and labor) to negotiate better prices...[16]

And as with all even partially competitive systems, companies take a risk if they don't grow as big and powerful as their rivals. McChesney also highlights vertical mergers, where firms buy their suppliers or distributors: "Vertical integration is a powerful stimulant to concentration; once a few firms in an industry move in this direction, others must follow suit or they can find themselves at an insurmountable competitive disadvantage— possibly blocked at all turns by opposing gatekeepers."[17] In the end, "As with oligopolistic markets in the broader economy, small independents exist to do the stuff the big guys find too risky or unprofitable. If successful, they tend to get bought out or enter into a formal dependent relationship with a giant."

So despite endless technological changes and mergers, the reach of the five largest firms still extends to nine in ten TV viewers.[18] And with so few firms, they tend to do a lot of business together—going in on new risky projects together, pooling capital for major investments, sharing risk and cementing their market power. And again, while "libertarian" economists theorize free markets are automatically competitive settings, industrial organization is recognized by the industry to be hugely important, even if they aggressively fight it among the workforce: "The top media moguls stay in constant touch, meeting annually in Idaho to discuss mutual interests and map future deals." Regarding Milton Friedman's most fundamental thesis, that markets permit consumers to be "free to choose," especially in this most important information market, McChesney's retort is "People can't reasonably express their desire for an alternative in the marketplace if the choice does not exist... The market can prove to be a quiet, but ruthless, commissar."[19]

However, while power exercised by government is obvious, as with the commissars of the totalitarian Soviet Union, market power can hide, as shown by Clear Channel's hundreds of "local" radio stations. As mentioned in Chapter 1, a common way that today's oligopolies manage their markets is through the illusion of competition through different brands and subsidiaries. As the *Journal* describes:

> Via a practice called 'voice-tracking,' Clear Channel pipes popular out-of-town personalities from bigger markets to small ones, customizing their programs to make it sound as if the DJs are actually local residents... It's also a huge benefit to Clear Channel, which can boast of a national reach and economies of scale to advertisers and shareholders... That's why Clear Channel is developing multiple identities for a battalion of DJs like the 29-year-old Mr. Alan, who is based at KHTS-FM in San Diego, but also does 'local' shows in Boise, Medford, Ore., and Santa Barbara, Calif.[20]

The conservative paper describes the legacy of deregulation:

> The new sound of radio is tied to big changes in the industry brought on by a 1996 law that got rid of the nationwide ownership cap of 40 stations. The law allowed companies to own as many as eight stations in the largest markets, double the previous limit... A fragmented business once made up mainly of mom-and-pop operators evolved quickly into one dominated by large publicly traded companies that controlled stations around the country. No one took advantage of the new law more aggressively, or successfully, than Clear Channel... Today, it operates more than 1,200 U.S. stations, compared with 186 stations owned by its biggest publicly traded rival, Viacom Inc.

This practice exists among local TV stations too, where the Pew Research Center found that in almost half of local US TV markets, recent mergers have "resulted in stations in the same market being separately owned on paper but operated jointly," a practice called "joint sales agreements."[21] These arrangements have contributed to the fact that a quarter of local TV stations now produce literally no original news content, with different media conglomerates sharing news vans and the totally hilarious practice of allegedly different stations airing literally identical programming. Pew observes that for owners, "The economic benefits of station consolidation are indisputable."

So once again, we have a few huge empires, unlike the diverse "free market" that the Right promises. However, the giant semi-monopolists are prepared to use some of their enormous resources to *look like* a rich and diverse industry, using faked "local" radio and outright duplicated TV programming. Meanwhile, the radio empire Clear Channel carries Rush Limbaugh and a parade of similar idiot radio hosts who put the blame for our economic problems on our "heavily regulated" economy. But the huge size and power of Clear Channel, their employer, is a direct result of the *deregulation* of radio and other media following the 1996 law. Irony loves company!

A similar pattern arises with the conservative Fox News, part of right-wing Australian billionaire Rupert Murdoch's News Corporation empire. The *Journal*, again, wrote that the Federal Communications Commission has for many decades maintained a "25% foreign-ownership limit on TV and radio stations... The FCC has long had the ability to waive the foreign-ownership cap for individual companies, but in practice has rarely used it. One of the few exceptions concerned Rupert Murdoch's News Corp."[22] Fox News, then, has built up its empire of feverish right-wing political reporting thanks to a (then) privileged exemption to the allegedly repressive-of-business power of the government. Yet, the channel still runs "Regulation Nation" segments, claiming that the economy's weak job market is caused by the government's rigid regulations, which were no obstacle to building its own empire. The *Journal* itself was bought by News Corporation in 2007, with libertarianism refuted by yet another of its own supporters.

The late *Washington Post* editor and media critic Ben Bagdikian has observed that today's media empire executives have "more communications power than was exercised by any despot or dictatorship in history."[23] And the industry has organized itself to serious effect:

> Though not a literal cartel like OPEC, the Big Five, in addition to cooperation with each other when it serves a mutual purpose, have interlocking members on their boards of directors... All five join forces in one of Washington's most powerful lobbies, the National Association of Broadcasters... The media conglomerates are not the only industry whose owners have become monopolistic in the American economy. But media products are unique in one vital respect. They do not manufacture nuts and bolts: they manufacture a social and political world.[24]

Bagdikian allows that "Some competition is never totally absent among the Big Five media conglomerates. The desire to be the first among many is as true for linked corporations as it is for politicians and nations,"[25] but that's still a far cry from the rich markets we were promised by the Right. It all means that the many sources of information in the reactionary dogma of the market are merely handsome hallucinations.

And as we've seen, the business press has itself spent years reporting on the dark reasons for this media consolidation. We read that:

> ... the new media giants have discovered that owning both broadcast and cable outlets provides powerful new leverage over advertisers and cable- and satellite-TV operators. The goliaths are using this advantage to wring better fees out of the operators that carry their channels and are pressuring those operators into carrying new and untried channels...

Media companies counter that their consolidation only puts them on a level playing field with cable operators, who are themselves merging into giants.[26]

On a more obvious level, the media-monitoring group FAIR reported the pathetic way the proposed Comcast-Time Warner merger was covered on Comcast's property, MSNBC. On the conservative show "Scarborough Country," the tough-talking conservative host brought up his boss, Comcast CEO Brian Roberts, as FAIR recounts:

> The merger also came up during a brief chat with Scarborough and business pundit Donny Deutsch. "We know Brian," Scarborough explained. "We get our paychecks from Comcast. Obviously we're not sort of cool and detached from this news." He added: "Even if I weren't working here... I would be saying, 'It's a pretty stunning story about how successful Comcast is right now.' Deutsch concurred: "Everything they've done is right."[27]

That's some hard-hitting reporting there, Scoop! Episodes like this have probably contributed to driving Americans' trust in commercial media down to all-time lows of 40 percent in recent years' Gallup polls.[28] And indeed, it's reasonable to say that when watching commercial media, you are watching concentrated money and corporate power speak to you, presenting the narrow range of ideas they'd like you to pay attention to. The "other companies" that the Friedmans alleged would "protect" us are about as protective as an absentee parent, and certainly no "positive freedom" is present here, which in this context would mean having freedom to access a wide variety of views from commercial and non-commercial sources.

Money Yells

So, with media corporation CEOs, business journalists and radical analysts all agreeing that media markets are highly concentrated and have only grown more so since deregulation, how do the big figures of right-wing economics deal with this departure from their models of free information flowing through diverse markets? It turns out, they really don't.

Milton Friedman briefly acknowledged limits to market information, such as prices, with his wife in *Free to Choose*: "Anything that prevents prices from expressing freely the conditions of demand or supply interferes with the transmission of accurate information. Private monopoly—control over a particular commodity by one producer or a cartel of producers—is one example. That does not prevent the transmission of information through the price system, but it does distort the information transmitted."[29] This could be a significant admission from Friedman, but almost unbelievably, the only example the Friedmans give of this potentially embarrassing point is OPEC, the global oil cartel made up of various governments, not private companies. So even when briefly acknowledging the possibility of market monopoly and the warping of market data, the Friedmans still can't bring themselves to mention a single example actually from the private sector. This allows them to dismiss the issue: "Important as private distortions of the price system are, these days the government is the major source of interference with a free market system." But the waves of consolidation and choice-reduction following media deregulation prove that breezily blowing past the issue of private power over information has not served the interests of freedom.

Hayek has an even stronger reputation on the Right as being a defender of freedom of information; however, his attitude toward the issue betrays his elitist view of humanity: "Probably it is true enough that the great majority are rarely capable of thinking independently, that on most questions they accept views which they find ready-made, and that they will be equally content if born or coaxed into one set of beliefs or another. In any society freedom of thought will probably be of direct significance only for a small minority."[30] Once again, the strong class bias of the political Right comes back, with the ugly we-were-meant-to-rule attitude of Ayn Rand and other fascists of capital.

However, Hayek continues: "But this does not mean that anyone is competent, or ought to have power, to select those to whom this freedom is to be reserved... It shows a complete confusion of thought to suggest that, because under any sort of system the majority of people follow the lead of somebody, it makes no difference if everybody has to follow the same lead." More to the point, Hayek also suggests that "the effect of propaganda in totalitarian countries is different not only in magnitude but in kind from that of the propaganda made for different ends by independent and competing agencies. If all the sources of current information are effectively under one single control, it is no longer a question of merely persuading the people of this or that." Hayek's argument is relevant for societies where state-run media dominate the information system, including not only more authoritarian regimes like China and Russia, but also pro-Western dictatorships like Saudi Arabia and Chad. But private media lead the world system and their limits are less discussed by Nobelists of Hayek's stripe.

Hayek's blissful lack of concern about propaganda by "independent and competing agencies" runs head-on into the work of figures like Edward Bernays, the pioneer of propaganda and public relations for both the state and for private capital. Bernays' long career among today's various power centers makes it difficult to accept the Friedmans' and Hayek's view that business has little propaganda power. He wrote that "It was, of course, the astounding success of propaganda during the war that opened the eyes of the intelligent few in all departments of life to the possibilities of regimenting the public mind... Business offers graphic examples of the effect that may be produced upon the public by interested groups."[31] And certainly the PR world brags about having "The Power to Change the Debate," quoting the web page of major DC firm Berman and Company.[32]

Bernays, clearly, is no less elitist than Hayek, but his experience working for the "invisible government" confirms the trend of concentration in media and information markets: "The invisible government tends to be concentrated in the hands of the few because of the expense of manipulating the social machinery which controls the opinions and habits of the masses." Hayek's insistence that state propaganda "is different not only in magnitude but in kind" from the widespread corporate use of similar tools is also addressed by Bernays: "New activities call for new nomenclature. The propagandist... has come to be known by the name of 'public relations counsel.'"[33] Bernays' point, obviously, was that these are fancy names for the same job.

In fact, Bernays also makes a direct connection between Friedman's and Hayek's assumption that free markets are rich, competitive and diverse sources of information, against the clear reality of oligopoly. He begins by noting that "The tendency of big business is to get bigger. Through mergers and monopolies it is constantly increasing the number of persons with whom it is in direct contact."[34] But often:

Public opinion is no longer inclined to be unfavorable to the large business merger. It resents the censorship of business by the Federal Trade Commission. It has broken down the anti-trust laws where it thinks they hinder economic development. It backs great trusts and mergers which it excoriated a decade ago... In the opinion of millions of small investors, mergers and trusts are friendly giants and not ogres, because of the economies, mainly due to quantity production, which they have effected, and can pass on to the consumer. This result has been, to a great extent, obtained by a deliberate use of propaganda in its broadest sense... But it would be rash and unreasonable to take it for granted that because public opinion has come over to the side of big business, it will always remain there.[35]

Tim Wu, a Columbia University professor of law and author of *The Master Switch*, maybe the best book on media and information industry concentration, described the inherent drive toward monopoly in network industries like media markets:

The defining principle of network economics is the so-called network effect, or network externality. It is the simple but powerful idea that unlike most products, a network becomes more valuable as more people use it. No one joins a social network like Facebook without other users. And a network that everyone uses is worth fantastically more than the sum value of one hundred networks with as many users collectively as the one great network.[36]

Friedman and Hayek's total failure to address an extremely basic feature of this important kind of market displays a lack of seriousness that is characteristic of their widely respected work. But these characters are still featured on today's conservative radio and TV shows, which themselves blame our economic problems on regulations, even though their own empire-building success is itself owed to removed or weakened regulation. Once again, whether their work was used to lower tax rates on the richest and most powerful US households, or to deregulate finance, media and food safety, these figures are Nobel Prize-winning intellectual opportunists.

Putting Their Money Where Your Mouth Is

The problems with the freedom of market information aren't limited to the tight ownership of the media markets, nor their network structure. The business model of the industry itself, in however many hands, also has an enormously important role in shaping the information that gets through.

James Curran's and Jean Seaton's book *Power Without Responsibility* is considered to be one of the most influential books on media history in the UK. Their review of the record shows that the concentration of the newspaper industry into a few huge publishers was indeed partially driven by the issues reviewed in Chapter 1, like network effects and scale economies arising from the rising cost of publishing equipment. This:

> ... rise in fixed costs made it more difficult for people with limited funds to break into mass publishing. It also generated a relationship of economic inequality, since leading publishers were able to obtain large economies of scale (through spreading their 'first copy' costs over a large print run)... The operation of the free market had raised the cost of press ownership beyond the readily available resources of the working class. Market forces thus accomplished more than the most repressive measures of an aristocratic state.[37]

However, it was the development of the advertising market itself that led to overwhelming market concentration and the loss of independent voices. As newspapers began reaching larger audiences, running paid advertisements from other commercial firms became possible. Part of this new ad revenue could be used to offset a lowered newspaper cover price, which further increased circulation for papers that attracted advertising. This gradually led to a few huge newspaper chains run by "press barons," because "nearly all newspapers... depended on advertising for their profits since their reduced net cover prices no longer met their costs. Advertisers thus acquired a de facto licensing power because, without their support, newspapers ceased to be economically viable."[38] And unsurprisingly, "Even non-socialist newspapers found that controversial editorial policies led to the loss of commercial advertising... Yet publications which conformed to the marketing requirements of advertisers obtained what were, in effect, large external subsidies which they could spend on increased editorial outlay and promotion in order to attract new readers." Thus, free-market forces *narrowed* the diversity of opinion in the media.

Of course, companies spending money on marketing prefer audiences with money to spend. For this reason, former *Washington Post* editor Bagdikian describes "an iron rule of advertising-supported media: It is less important that people buy your publication (or listen to your program) than that they be 'the right kind' of people. The 'right kind' usually means affluent consumers eighteen to forty-nine years of age, the heavy buying years, with above-median family income."[39] Also, advertisers "are increasingly interested in the context of their ads in the medium — the surrounding articles in newspapers and magazines and the type of broadcast program in which their commercials are inserted. An ad for a sable fur coat next to an article on world starvation is not the most effective association for making a sale."

It was in this spirit that ABC put out a booklet for its advertisers, as an industry journal, *Broadcasting*, described some years ago: "ABC-TV has presented advertisers with a new prime time sales booklet that contains a section arguing that ABC not only has the biggest audiences but the most desirable demographics as well. The section is labeled, 'Some people are more valuable than others.'" NBC's programming head retorted that ABC's viewers were more numerous but had lower incomes, concluding "their audience will be worthless."[40]

The sleazy ways this plays out on the air today are vigilantly reviewed by FAIR, including in its annual "Fear & Favor Review," which documents how the media firms' owners and advertisers warp and shape the information that reaches the average citizen. The 2013 Review pointed out a *Washington Post* "debate" on energy policy, which "featured proponents of oil and gas drilling, but no industry critics, perhaps because it was derived from forums co-sponsored by Vote4Energy.org, a project of the American Petroleum Institute. *Post* readers weren't alerted to that fact," though it was referred to in an online video.[41]

The power of market institutions makes itself felt elsewhere, even in market segments that seem to be based on delivering very objective information. Consider ratings services — firms that measure some process or trend and produce reports summarizing them. Recently, Volkswagen dominated headlines for its faked emission readings, but in fact the issue is systemic. *The Wall Street Journal* describes "a system in which car makers pay the very firms that test and certify their vehicles. That system relies on the use of so-called 'golden vehicles,' stripped down prototypes that car makers send to testing firms for inspection."[42] This "widespread" and "cozy" relationship "allows car models to undergo tests before they are fitted with everything from back seats to wheels with heavier tread, boosting fuel efficiency and lowering emissions." The article cites European critics suggesting "the commercial ties between car makers and testing firms allow them to wield too much influence over test results," with an environmental group in Brussels saying "There is no incentive to be tough on car makers."

A further example of commercial power and its limiting impact on the market can be found in Gloria Steinem's description of the difficulty in securing advertisers for the feminist *Ms. Magazine* in its early days:

When *Ms.* began, we didn't consider not taking ads. The

most important reason was keeping the price of a feminist magazine low enough for most women to afford... Food advertisers have always demanded that women's magazines publish recipes and articles on entertaining (preferably ones that name their products) in return for their ads; clothing advertisers expect to be surrounded by fashion spreads (especially ones that credit their designers); and shampoo, fragrance, and beauty products in general usually insist on positive editorial coverage of beauty subjects, plus photo credits besides. That's why women's magazines look the way they do.[43]

An especially embarrassing example comes from *The Wall Street Journal* itself, the prominent conservative business paper that has for years excellently documented the problems caused by market deregulation, while arguing for even more of it on the editorial page. In February 2008, the paper ran an editorial about the then emerging financial crisis, focusing on the credit-rating companies Standard & Poor's (S&P), Moody's and Fitch, whose job is to rate financial products, like bonds, in terms of their expected yield and risk. These "Big Three" agencies became notorious for granting very safe "AAA" ratings to the highly risky subprime mortgage securities issued during the housing bubble. The *Journal* editors claimed this was because government regulators had prevented other firms from entering the market (until 2006), which would have encouraged more competition and rating honesty. However, the bigger issue is the basic business model—the rating agencies make far more money if they grant high ratings to junky "subprime" assets, because the large investment banks and financial firms selling them are willing to pay for these favorable ratings, creating an "issuer pays" model.

The *Journal* leaves the blame on the SEC, but apparently has no problem with the issue of being paid by the companies whose products you're supposed to evaluate. The paper does acknowledge the issue: "But every business has potential conflicts. In the newspaper industry, we sell ads to the same people we cover. The question is how firms manage these conflicts—and whether the marketplace is allowed to discipline companies that fail investors."[44] Indeed, in an official corporate reply on the editorial page a week later, an S&P official said "Reputable news outlets like the *Journal* keep a strict 'church and state' separation between their editorial and business operations. Similarly at S&P, we have rigorous policies to support the independence of our ratings..."[45] This debate is interesting and revealing, since both business media like the *Journal* and credit-rating agencies like S&P are important parts of modern information markets.

First, the marketplace has indeed disciplined S&P, but not quite how the *Journal* editors expected. They would probably agree with Hayek, that the information relevant to these financial securities would be most accurate if supplied by the market. And indeed, after the crisis, the Big Three were chastened by their catastrophic rating biases and tightened up their criteria. S&P stiffened its rating criteria the most, but then found it was losing market share—since in the marketplace, making money means being hired by the firms whose securities they are supposed to judge impartially. But this meant S&P's business suffered relative to the other firms as it assigned lower ratings to financial products, and eventually the firm announced it was "introducing modified business standards that made it easier to give bonds higher ratings," as the business press described.

> The changes seemed to work. More banks began choosing S.& P. to rate the new bonds backed by residential mortgages... Since S.& P. eased its standards last year, its market share has risen to 69 percent from the 18 percent it had in the first years after the crisis... On nearly every deal since it changed its standards, S.& P. has been willing to make more optimistic

predictions about the bonds it was rating than the other agencies rating the deals... Bankers want more optimistic predictions because they make the bonds easier to sell to investors.[46]

So the "market discipline" is *not* to share real information accurately, as Hayek insisted would happen, but to supply the *right* information—that which is most conducive to immediate profit-making.

Secondly, this "church and state separation" between newspaper ad departments and editorial offices isn't very impressive, and the *Journal* itself has let its own ad-driven business model take priority over its alleged integrity. The advertising industry's trade magazine, *Advertising Age*, has reported on the huge growth of "sponsored content," which is material paid for and supplied by outside companies but set up to *look* like regular news coverage.

By wrapping ad messages in a format that looks like editorial content—and calling them something else, such as 'sponsored' or 'partner' content—they hope to trade on the trust and goodwill editorial has built up with the audience... *The Wall Street Journal* publishes three special sections underwritten by Deloitte [the financial services giant]... where editorial stories by *Journal* reporters run alongside a box of content marked as sponsored. Deloitte has no influence over which editorial stories appear, a *Wall Street Journal* spokeswoman said.[47]

These same principles definitely also apply to the *Journal*'s corporate parent, News Corporation. The network blames regulation and big government for society's problems, but in 1998, journalists for a Fox-owned Florida TV station prepared a story on a synthetic hormone designed to increase milk production in cows, produced by Monsanto, the enormous manufacturer of Roundup weedkiller and other commercial chemicals. The journalists found that the hormone caused serious health problems in the cows and was likely to affect milk drinkers hormonally, despite the FDA's approval of the drug (more on this rubber-stamp nature of current regulation in Chapter 3).

As the excellent *PR Watch* reports, "Immediately after FDA approval of rBGH, attorneys for Monsanto sued or threatened to sue stores and dairy companies that sold milk and dairy products advertised as being free of rBGH," usually for "defamation."[48] But Monsanto threatened Fox with "dire consequences," presumably in the form of withdrawn advertising and legal suits. The network's own legal staff dragged the journalists through dozens of revisions, attempting to minimize or remove any mention of cancer or other specific health effects. Bribes and bullying were also attempted, including an episode where the journalists claimed a manager said "We paid $3 billion for these television stations. We will decide what the news is. The news is what we tell you it is."

Hayek claims the market is an "efficient mechanism for digesting dispersed information." Meanwhile, we're digesting synthetic cow hormones.

Original Spin

These pressures, from concentrated corporate ownership and an advertising revenue-based business model, mean that freedom of information is often very constrained in a market system. The resulting media performance has been analyzed by radical media critics Edward Herman and Noam Chomsky, whose classic book *Manufacturing Consent* organized the various market and institutional pressures on news into a simple "Propaganda Model," built around the different filters that shape and limit the information received by the man on the street. One filter is "the limitation on ownership of media with any substantial outreach by the requisite large size of investment," which means the media tend to be "owned and controlled by quite wealthy people" who "have a special stake in the status quo by virtue of their wealth and their strategic position in one of the great institutions of society."[49] Likewise with the filtering power of advertising capital in the market:

> With advertising, the free market does not yield a neutral system in which final buyer choice decides. The *advertiser's* choices influence media prosperity and survival... The power of advertisers over television programming stems from the simple fact they buy and pay for the programs—they are the 'patrons' who provide the media subsidy. As such, the media compete for their patronage.[50]

Elsewhere, Chomsky used a revealing paired example to explore the pro-status quo features of the capitalist media marketplace, with regard to aggressive US foreign policy:

> We have no problem in perceiving the Soviet invasion of Afghanistan as brutal aggression... But the U.S. invasion of South Vietnam in the early 1960s, when the Latin American-style terror state imposed by U.S. force could no longer control the domestic population by violence, cannot be perceived as it was. True, U.S. forces were directly engaged in large-scale bombing and defoliation in an effort to drive the population into concentration camps where they could be "protected" from the enemy whom, it was conceded, they willingly supported. True, a huge U.S. expeditionary force later invaded and ravaged the country, and its neighbors, with the explicit aim of destroying what was clearly recognized to be the only mass-based political force... But throughout,

the United States was resisting aggression in its yearning for democracy.[51]

Herman wrote that a merit of this system, from the point of view of the powerful:

> ... is that it is not total and responds with some flexibility to the differences that frequently crop up among elite groups. This allows controversy to rage within the mass media, but confined almost completely to tactical matters... In sum, a market system of control limits free expression largely by market processes that are highly effective. Dissident ideas are not legally banned, they are simply unable to reach mass audiences.[52]

This is also the basis for the use of commercial media in this book, since the information in the national press, like *The Wall Street Journal* and *The New York Times*, is excellent but limited to conventional views of the social system. So rising wealth inequality, aggravated instability and indeed media ownership concentration are reported in these media, but within a limited range that stops short of suggesting these issues are symptoms of problems with our economic system. Much as with the foreign policy coverage Chomsky describes above, the commercial media very often provide valuable information, especially in their business sections for investors and executives who need good data, but within specific limits.

Edward Bernays, the PR pioneer who believed in cooperation between business and government, had his own thoughts about the resulting media performance:

> ... it remains a fact that in almost every act of our daily lives... we are dominated by the relatively small number of persons... In some departments of our daily life, in which we imagine

ourselves free agents, we are led by dictators exercising great power. A man buying a suit of clothes imagines that he is choosing, according to his taste and his personality, the kind of garment he prefers. In reality, he may be obeying the orders of an anonymous gentleman tailor in London.[53]

While Friedman said we are Free to Choose, actual PR cofounder Bernays said we are in fact Free to Imagine That We Choose.

It's also worth addressing the relentlessly repeated claim by conservative media that the media generally are "liberal." This claim is about as bedrock as you can get on the Right, and is usually based (if any evidence is given at all) on the tendency of journalists and editors to vote for the Democratic Party. Herman notes that this argument avoids:

> ... the questions of ownership and control, implying that lower echelon personnel set their own agendas, without rules from above. The massive historic evidence that key owners... have had definite policy agendas that they have enforced in their organizations is simply not discussed... The neo-conservative analysts also don't do much in the way of analyzing actual news and opinion outputs. Their main focus is on whether the reporters and copy editors vote Republican or Democratic.[54]

The definitive mid-century writer on freedom of expression and against state control of thought is George Orwell, whose *Animal Farm* and *1984* became popular classics on the dangers of control of knowledge by tyrannical governments. Indeed, Orwell's books are even frequently seen in libertarian book catalogs. However, Orwell also wrote a preface to *Animal Farm* that went unpublished in the UK for decades, in which he made his point clear that control over information was not purely a state-power phenomenon:

The sinister fact about literary censorship in England is that it is largely voluntary. Unpopular ideas can be can be silenced, and inconvenient facts kept dark, without the need for any official ban... not because the Government intervened but because of a general tacit agreement that 'it wouldn't do' to mention that particular fact. So far as the daily newspapers go, this is easy to understand. The British press is extremely centralized, and most of it is owned by wealthy men who have every motive to be dishonest on certain important topics. But the same kind of veiled censorship also operates in books and periodicals, as well as in plays, films and radio. At any given moment there is an orthodoxy, a body of ideas which it is assumed that all right-thinking people will accept without question... Anyone who challenges the prevailing orthodoxy finds himself silenced with surprising effectiveness. A genuinely unfashionable opinion is almost never given a fair hearing, either in the popular press or in the highbrow periodicals.[55]

This part of Orwell's work, claiming capitalism suppresses freedom of information, hasn't received the same media attention as his work criticizing the USSR. For some reason.

TMI Inc.

So the media markets that bring us information are warped by tightly concentrated ownership and by their advertising revenue-based business model. But the scale of the advertising itself, and the scale of data collection carried out by firms to refine it, are also important for understanding how markets restrict and limit our freedom of information. The relentless character of modern marketing can be seen in the estimate by advertising professionals that urban consumers saw about 2000 ads a day in 1970, with today's figure closer to a staggering 5000 daily. Ad firms boast to the business press that successful marketing is "in your face, and you can blanket a marketplace."[56] This refers to the virtually unlimited scope of modern advertising, on TV, in print, online, on hold, before movies, during movies, pasted to the pharmacy floor, sprayed onto food, projected onto buildings, posted by the road, played on the radio, painted on cars, worked into ball games and written in the sky. And a growing market segment is engaged in marketing to kids, before their critical thinking powers even have a chance to kick in. One freedom you do not have is freedom from constant advertising messages.

This ubiquity definitely includes the school system, where young people are supposed to be introduced to ideas and information in their formative years, and where "brands have managed, over the course of only one decade, to all but eliminate the barrier between ads and education," as Naomi Klein put it.[57] Public budgets have fallen, typically including education cuts, and "As fast-food, athletic gear and computer companies step in to fill the gap, they carry with them an educational agenda all their own." Bagdikian also notes that "Free classroom materials are produced by 64 percent of the five hundred largest American industrial corporations, 90 percent of industrial trade associations, and 90 percent of utility companies."[58]

Besides the relentless bombarding of consumers and students with commercial information to shape views and drive consumption, firms have for some time also used these media properties to directly improve their own image in the eyes of the public. This practice has evolved since Bernays' time—in 2012, *The Times* described the fast-food chain McDonald's as "quietly launching a major counteroffensive" against its critics among the movement for better nutrition, with a company plan to "change how we *think* about food." The power to do this depends on money, but the chain is up to the challenge: it spends $2 billion a year on marketing, enough to fully immunize 10 million African children each year.[59] Because McDonalds "owns nearly

17 percent of the limited-service restaurant industry," equal to the next four largest chains combined, it can "reach an audience far larger than the one that saw 'Super Size Me,'" and pay to keep its stories at the top of the Twitter trends list, showing how today's celebrated "grassroots social media" are just as readily manipulated by money as the older media they succeeded.

However, a more cutting-edge aspect of marketing is what McDonald's calls "brand work." In the face of spreading consumer demand for healthier food, the company aims to distort the (accurate) perception that its processed food is unhealthy: "In exchange for perks like free trips, access to important people and sometimes financial compensation, bloggers are encouraged or even contractually bound to write about a company... Some bloggers... get paid as much as $20,000 for the work, which by McDonald's ad-campaign standards isn't much money." But entrepreneurs find it's effective at keeping consumers swallowing McDonald's.

The brand work is designed for "reaching an audience that has become wary of slick ad campaigns," since the ad comes not from the company itself but "from somebody they trust," as an expert puts it. For stressed blue- and white-collar mothers, receiving a five-figure payment for a lowly blog post, or being flown to meet high-ranking corporate officials, is a major event, even if invisibly cheap for McDonald's colossal marketing budget. A "mom blogger" describes how after meeting company president Jan Fields, "Now I relate to her... and in turn I relate to McDonald's." This paid promotion of favorable information is another violation of the pretty picture of automatic information transmission put up by the defenders of capitalist markets, like Hayek, and reveals vital information to be a plaything of the ruling class.

Indeed, the social media themselves are generally good examples of the power of money to warp the information we receive, as on Twitter where fake accounts can be bought by the thousands for about six cents each at current prices, *The Wall Street Journal* reports.[60] Similar to this is the genre of TV and online ads, where hardworking employees of a giant conglomerate (or good-looking actors portraying them) appear on camera saying, "I'm Company X." The intention is clear: repeat a message associating the company with normal working people, not a large corporate institution with unpopular policies.

But these efforts to shape our perception of firms are only one side of the coin. The other side has to do with how firms collect data to fine-tune promotions, which means gathering information. In this era of huge public concern about data gathering and privacy, the focus is almost entirely on the PATRIOT ACT and the National Security Agency's PRISM data collection, which have become correctly notorious for their apparently almost universal hoarding of personal communications. But the practice has also become a mainstay of the corporate world, where giant concentrated resources again create real social power.

Before today's online economy, where a product viewed one moment becomes an ad following you around the Web, the large US retailers led the wave of private collection of personal data in order to tailor sales pitches—and without the consumer's awareness that this is happening. Profiling Target as a leader in modern data-driven marketing, *The New York Times* reports that firms can "buy data" about virtually any aspect of your work history, consumption profile, or even social and political views.[61] In fact, the only drawback so far for retailers is how well their data collection works, risking a "public-relations" disaster if women, for example, found out Target knew they were pregnant before their family did.

The company ultimately developed a poker face, where Target "camouflaged how much it knew," in order to encourage new shopping habits in customers going through life changes, to the point where an executive confides "we started mixing in all these ads for things we knew pregnant women would never buy, so the baby ads looked random." The program represents an enormous "informational asymmetry," where one side of a deal knows more than the other side. The manufacturer knows more about the quality of a good than a new consumer and a worker knows their own work ethic better than an employer. Target and other retailers investing their giant resources in data are considered to have achieved mixed success, and similar methods have been used by other large consumer goods firms like Proctor & Gamble. The Target corporation ultimately told their statistician to stop communicating with the press, perhaps concerned they had tipped the industry's hand.

At this point, we should refer again to the view of Milton and Rose Friedman on this subject. They wrote in *Free to Choose*:

> What about the claim that consumers can be led by the nose by advertising? Our answer is that they can't—as numerous expensive advertising fiascos testify. One of the greatest duds of all time was the Edsel automobile, introduced by Ford Motor Company and promoted by a major advertising campaign. More basically, advertising is a cost of doing business, and the businessman wants to get the most for this money. Is it not more sensible to try to appeal to the real wants and desires of consumers than to try to manufacture artificial wants or desires? Surely it will generally be cheaper to sell them something that meets wants they already have than to create an artificial want... The real objection of most critics of advertising is not that advertising manipulates tastes but that the public at large has meretricious tastes—that is, tastes that do not agree with the critics.[62]

"They can't." But they quite commonly do, as shown above. The fact that it sometimes fails doesn't mean it's not brainwashing; Soviet propaganda was by no means universally believed, so does that mean that it wasn't relentless propaganda capable of having a cumulative effect? And if "artificially-creating desires" is futile, it's hard to explain Coca-Cola spending about $3 billion on marketing its chemical-syrup water every year, while Pepsi clocks $2 billion annually, according to *Advertising Age*.[63] It's unlikely that this pair of firms are throwing away $5 billion of good profit every year even though "They can't" have any influence over consumer behavior. But according to the dean of conservative economics, we don't *really* think advertising manipulates people. We're just snobs. Case closed!

Then, when city and state governments try passing taxes on sugary drinks because of their socially expensive health impacts, the beverage industry (through their own organized trade body, the American Beverage Association) hires canvassers to go door-to-door opposing the restrictions, wearing shirts saying "I picked out my beverage all by myself." The message of course is that governments making sugary drinks more costly is paternalistic—it treats people like children. However, the ABA's member companies tend to outspend political opponents ten-to-one, flooding media with one-sided information.[64] The fact is that you did not choose your beverage yourself, Coke drinker—corporations threw a lot of valuable capital at your attention span while you watched TV as a child and an adult, to cultivate non-rational attachments and associations in your mind with their sugary beverages.

Stuart Ewen, author of the classic book *Captains of Consciousness*, has engaged in careful scholarship to document the business thinking that went into this ad-swamped world of today. He cites business economist Paul Nystrom, who said the dull, monotonous aspect of work under industrial capitalism was creating a "philosophy of futility," which could itself stimulate more consumption: "this lack of purpose in life has an effect on consumption similar to that of having a narrow life interest, that is, in concentrating human attention on the more superficial things that comprise much of fashionable consumption."[65] This is quite beyond Friedman's simple view and indeed it's more often the powerful market execs who have the snobby attitudes. Whether the market is for shoes, cars or healthcare, the free-market phenomena of concentration and class interest put power in the hands of a few giant empires and their wealthy owners. But in information markets, the stakes are far higher, limiting the very ideas we're exposed to and blocking the social change that could try to deal with these power centers. While we value freedom of information, our market system is more concerned with its quarterly profit results. In the market of ideas, money yells louder than words.

Price tags for shaping the marketplace of ideas[66]

Blogger praise online	$20,000
Economist papers favoring financial deregulation	$124,000
Place a book on *The New York Times* bestseller list through PR agency buys	$210,000
A House election campaign, deciding idea dominance in policy	$650,000
Olympics Partnership, allowing an on-site pavilion and prestige used in ads	$100 million
Buy *The Washington Post*	$250 million
Global annual ad campaign keeping brands in front of consumers	$3 billion

Endnotes

1. Albert Einstein, "Why Socialism?" *Monthly Review*, May 1949.

2. Alex Carey, *Taking the Risk Out of Democracy*, Champaign, IL: University of Illinois Press, 1997, p. 18.

3. John Stuart Mill, *On Liberty*, Mineola, NY: Dover, 2002, p. 14.

4. Friedrich Hayek, Nobel Prize Lecture, "The Pretence of Knowledge," 11 December 1974.

5. Edward Bernays, *Public Relations*, Norman, OK: University of Oklahoma Press, 1952, p. 78; *Propaganda*, Brooklyn: Ig Publishing, 2005, p. 37.

6. Friedrich Hayek, *The Road to Serfdom*, Chicago: University of Chicago Press, 2007, p. 178.

7. R. Glenn Hubbard and Anthony Patrick O'Brien, *Microeconomics*, New York: Pearson, 4th ed, p.54.

8. Milton and Rose Friedman, *Free to Choose*, New York: Harcourt, 1990, p. 13–5.

9. Friedrich Hayek, "The Use of Knowledge in Society," *American Economic Review*, Vol. 35, No. 4, September 1945.

10. "Labor Almost Invisible on TV Talk," FAIR, 28 August 2014.

11. U.S. Census Bureau, "Economic Census 2007," 2014.

12. U.S. House of Representatives, 104th Congress, 2nd Session, House Report 104–458, p. 1.

13. Deborah Solomon and Robert Frank, "Broad Bands: Comcast Deal Cements Rise of an Oligopoly In the Cable Business,"*The Wall Street Journal*, 21 December 2001.

14. Martin Peers, "Show of Strength: How Media Giants Are Reassembling the Old Oligopoly,"*The Wall Street Journal*, 15 September 2003.

15. Deborah Solomon and Robert Frank, "Broad Bands: Comcast Deal Cements Rise of an Oligopoly In the Cable Business,"*The Wall Street Journal*, 21 December 2001.

16. Robert McChesney, *The Problem of the Media*, New York: Monthly Review Press, 2004, p. 177.

17. *Ibid*, p. 180, 186.

18. *Ibid*, p. 183, 186.

19. *Ibid*, p. 202, 190.

20. Anna Mathews, "From a Distance: A Giant Radio Chain Is Perfecting the Art of Seeming Local,"*The Wall Street Journal*, 25 February 2002.

21. Pew Research Center, "Acquisitions and Content Sharing Shapes Local TV News in 2013," 16 March 2014.

22. Gautham Nagesh, "FCC Relaxes Rules on Foreign Ownership," *The Wall Street Journal*, 15 November 2013.

23. Ben Bagdikian, *The New Media Monopoly*, Boston: Beacon Press, 2002, p. 3.

24. *Ibid*, p. 8–9.

25. Ben Bagdikian, *The New Media Monopoly*, Boston: Beacon Press, 2002, p. 5–7, 50.

26. Martin Peers, "Show of Strength: How Media Giants Are Reassembling the Old Oligopoly," *The Wall Street Journal*, 15 September 2003.

27. "Our Boss Is Great! How MSNBC Covered Comcast Merger," Fair Blog, 19 February 2014.

28. Justin McCarthy, "Trust in Mass Media Returns to All-Time Low," Gallup, 17 September 2014.

29. Milton and Rose Friedman, *Free to Choose*, New York: Harcourt, 1980, p. 16–7.

30. Friedrich Hayek, *The Road to Serfdom*, Chicago: University of Chicago Press, 2007, p. 179.

31. Edward Bernays, *Propaganda*, Brooklyn: Ig Publishing, 2005, p. 54–5.

32. Berman and Compnay, http://www.bermanco.com/, accessed 29 November 2014.

33. Bernays, *Propaganda*, p. 63.

34. *Ibid*, p. 90.

35. *Ibid*, p. 94.

36. Tim Wu, *The Master Switch*, New York: Vintage, 2011, p. 318.

37. James Curran and Jean Seaton, *Power Without Responsibility*, London: Routledge, 2009, p. 26–8.

38. *Ibid*, p. 28-32.

39. Ben Bagdikian, *The New Media Monopoly*, Boston: Beacon Press, 2002, p. 223, 230.

40. "Not who's got the most; who's got the best?" *Broadcasting*,

9 January 1978.

41. "13th Annual Fear & Factor Review," *Extra!*, February 2013.

42. Jason Chow, Ruth Bender and David Gauthier-Villars, "Europe's Cozy Car Testing,"*The Wall Street Journal*, 1 October 2015.

43. Gloria Steinem, "Sex, Lies, & Advertising," *Ms. Magazine*, July/August 1990, p. 18–28.

44. "AAA Oligopoly,"*The Wall Street Journal*, 26 February 2008.

45. Vickie Tillman, "Standard & Poor's Gives Its Side of the Story,"*The Wall Street Journal*, 8 March 2008.

46. Nathanial Popper, "S.&P. Bond Deals Are on the Rise Since It Relaxed Rating Criteria,"*The New York Times* Dealbook, 17 September 2003.

47. "News Organizations Face Tricky Trade-Off With 'Sponsored Content,'" *Advertising Age*, 23 September 2013.

48. "Monsanto and Fox: Partners in Censorship," *PR Watch*, April-June 1998.

49. Edward Herman and Noam Chomsky, *Manufacturing Consent*, New York: Pantheon, 1988, p. 4–5, 8.

50. *Ibid*, p. 14, 16–7.

51. Noam Chomsky, *Necessary Illusions*, Boston: South End Press, 1989, p. 50.

52. Edward Herman, *Triumph of the Market*, Boston: South End Press, 1995, p. 171–2.

53. Edward Bernays, *Propaganda*, Brooklyn: Ig Publishing, 2005, p. 37–8, 61.

54. Edward Herman, *Triumph of the Market*, Boston: South End Press, 1995, p. 258, n. 8.

55. George Orwell, "The Freedom of the Press," *The Times Literary Supplement*, 15 September 1972.

56. Louise Story, "Anywhere the Eye Can see, It's Likely to See an Ad,"*The New York Times*, 15 January 2007.

57. Naomi Klein, *No Logo*, Picador: New York, 2002, p. 9.

58. Ben Bagdikian, *The New Media Monopoly*, Boston: Beacon

Press, 2002, p. 167.

59. Keith O'Brien, "How McDonald's Came Back Bigger Than Ever,"*The New York Times*, 4 May 2012.

60. Jeff Elder, "Inside a Twitter Robot Factory,"*The Wall Street Journal*, 24 November 2013.

61. Charles Duhigg, "How Companies Learn Your Secrets,"*The New York Times*, 16 February 2012.

62. Milton and Rose Friedman, *Free to Choose*, New York: Harcourt, 1990, p. 224–5.

63. Natalie Zmuda, "Pepsi plays catch-up with Coke, adds $556m in spending," *Advertising Age*, 29 January 2012.

64. Michael Grynbaum, "Soda Makers Begin Their Push Against New York Ban,"*The New York Times*, 1 July 2012; Vauhini Vara, "Campaign Over Soda Tax Bubbles Up,"*The Wall Street Journal*, 13 August 2012.

65. Stuart Ewen, *Captains of Consciouness*, New York: Basic Books, 2001, p. 85.

66. Keith O'Brien, "How McDonald's Came Back Bigger Than Ever,"*The New York Times*, 4 May 2012; Charles Ferguson, *Inside Job*, Sony Pictures Classics, 2011; Ruth Graham, "Can Megachurches Deal With Mega Money in a Christian Way?" *The Atlantic*, 12 March 2014; "Price of Admission," Center For Responsive Politics, https://www.opensecrets.org/bigpicture/stats.php?cycle=2012&type=A&display=A;David Segal, "In Olympic Park, a Deluge From Our Sponsors,"*The New York Times*, 11 August 2012; Brad Stone, "Why Jeff Bezos Bought *The Washington Post*," *Bloomberg Businessweek*, 8 August 2013; Natalie Zmuda, "Pepsi plays catch-up with Coke, adds $556m in spending," *Advertising Age*, 29 January 2012.

Chapter 3

Codependence Day
Political Freedom

Any honest Democrat will admit that we are all now Friedmanites.

Larry Summers[1]

A nation that continues year after year to spend more money on military defense than on programs of social uplift is approaching spiritual death.

Martin Luther King[2]

After the havoc of 2016, with the rule-breaking Sanders and Trump campaigns in the US, Brexit and broader skepticism about the European Union, rising authoritarianism in Turkey and Mexico, and governments wracked with corruption from Brazil to Malaysia, and above all the Trump administration, no one can doubt that popular disgust with politics has become more deeply felt and more globally prevalent in recent years. And with good reason—the level of cynicism shown by political figures, the divergence of official state policy from the basic desires of citizens and a pronounced movement toward more authoritarian government with wider surveillance, all add to the mountain of grievances felt around the world.

So it's interesting to see what the recent trends have been in government policy and where today's very unpopular "neoliberal" political trajectory has come from. Policy changes always require intellectual justification and here we return to the prominent libertarian figures whose work has been a focus of this book. Friedman and Hayek are especially identified with the beginnings and rationales for neoliberalism, since the very start of our "Age of Friedman," as the conservative *National Review* called it. So let's review how they see the issue.

Minority Rules

Conservatives and libertarians are strongly identified with supporting "smaller government," and the Friedmans' *Free to Choose* expounded on this at length:

Currently, more than 40 percent of our income is disposed of on our behalf by government at federal, state, and local levels combined. One of us once suggested a new national holiday, "Personal Independence Day—that day in the year when we stop working to pay the expenses of government... and start working to pay for the items we severally and individually choose in light of our own needs and desires." In 1929 that holiday would have come on Abraham Lincoln's birthday, February 12; today it would come about May 30; if present trends were to continue, it would coincide with the other Independence Day, July 4, around 1988.[3]

Of course, tax collections aren't mainly used to pay "the expenses of government," but to supply "public goods"—services that tend to be drastically underproduced by markets because they benefit the broader society, more than individuals. Things like roads, streetlights, bridges, sanitation systems and scientific research are examples, and the Friedmans do acknowledge this later: "City streets and general-access highways could be provided by private voluntary exchange, the costs being paid for by charging tolls. But the costs of collecting the tolls would often be very large compared to the cost of building and maintaining the streets or highways."[4] Likewise, services like education or immunization against diseases benefit everyone by yielding better educated societies that can provide more sophisticated goods and services, or a lower incidence of infectious diseases that benefits everyone in the society.

Notably, more consistent libertarians, like US economist Murray Rothbard, insist that even local roads could be efficiently run on a toll basis. He wrote in *Man, Economy and State* that "such services as education, road building and maintenance, coinage, postal delivery, fire protection, police protection, judicial decisions, and military defense" should be private and were "historically supplied by private enterprise."[5] Indeed, Rothbard and other more libertarian figures have disputed the very existence of public goods themselves. In the "Age of Friedman," the beginning of Rothbard's dream has come to pass, as a deadlocked US Congress has failed to pass the gas tax increases to pay for public road upkeep, forcing states to institute tolls on more and more roads – the US toll road mileage rose to 5400 miles, *The Wall Street Journal* reported.[6]

The rise of the Trump administration looks set to increase this trend, as the campaign promise of $1 trillion in infrastructure spending "relies entirely on private financing," the business press relates, "which industry experts say is likely to fall far short of adequately funding improvements to roads, bridges and airports."[7] This is likely difficult for Rand readers and supporters of libertarian purists like Rothbard to comprehend, but even sympathetic business media find the plan hard to buy. Since the proposal "largely boils down to a tax break in the hopes of luring capital to projects," problems arise as "Experts say there are limits to how much can be done with private financing. Because privately funded projects need to turn a profit, they are better suited for major projects such as toll roads, airports or water systems and less appropriate for routine maintenance, they say." Indeed, even the head of the business association representing private toll-road operators finds the plan more conceptual than serious. The paper also adds that "tolls have proved unpopular, with toll-road operators in Indiana and Texas filing for bankruptcy protection."

More fundamentally, critics of these libertarian views could argue that control over transport routes was the exact extortion opportunity used by German nobles that created the actual phrase "robber baron," now often applied to great capitalists. Much as at that time, private toll roads would leave drivers helpless before a multitude of local road barons—the *Journal* notes as an example that the city of Plano, Texas, is "nearly surrounded by toll roads." Perhaps a Toll Road to Serfdom.

But the Friedmans' point is that while a very limited number of social functions are indeed best provided collectively through public policy, government can still force people to comply, and therefore has power and ought to be sharply constrained. That's a reasonable principle, considering the "negative freedom" supported by these figures—the freedom from being made to do something by outside forces. But as we saw in Chapter 1, this kind of coercive power is prevalent in the market also.

Nonetheless, libertarians tend to see raw, violent coercion in even the most tame and sensible programs of public provision, if they tend to reduce the power of commercial institutions in the marketplace. One memorable instance appeared in one of Milton Friedman's columns for *Newsweek*, where he wrote this gem of Reaganite righteousness:

> "Consider social security. The young have always contributed to the support of the old. Earlier, the young helped their own parents out of a sense of love and duty. They now contribute to the support of someone else's parents out of compulsion and fear. The voluntary transfers strengthened the bonds of the family; the compulsory transfers weaken those bonds."[8]
> Yep, fear of the dark storm troopers of Social Security has torn our families asunder. And of course, with no public pensions, if a person makes a bad investment with their savings and loses it all, and lacks prosperous young relations, there's no safety net to prevent street grandmas.

But as has come up previously in this book, Friedman and Hayek, although the most prominent of conservative-libertarian economists, were also political advisers focused on what was achievable by their Reagan-Thatcher patrons. So Friedman, rather than the mass privatization of roadways that Rothbard supported, put his focus on social security or health regulations — easier targets for immediate policy change. Hayek, moreover, wrote for a Western European audience, which meant that the overwhelming popularity of public programs and welfare had to be accommodated: "Thus neither the provision of signposts on the roads nor, in most circumstances, that of the roads themselves can be paid for by every individual user," he said.[9] "Nor is the preservation of competition incompatible with an extensive system of social services," leaving "a wide and unquestioned field for state activity."[10] It's certainly questioned by American libertarians, who tend to be more purist, like Rothbard above.

The Friedmans also concede that in a republic, government is not based on a distant king's decrees but decided through some form of popular election:

> Of course, we have something to say about how much of our income is spent on our behalf by government. We participate in the political process that has resulted in government's spending an amount equal to more than 40 percent of our income. Majority rule is a necessary and desirable expedient. It is, however, very different from the kind of freedom you have when you shop at a supermarket. When you enter the voting booth once a year, you almost always vote for a package rather than for specific items... When you vote daily in the supermarket, you get precisely what you voted for, and so does everyone else.[11]

The Friedmans are again merely presuming a rich, diverse and competitive marketplace, which as we saw in Chapter 1 isn't so common. That chapter also reviewed how this picture of "voting" with your dollars in the market, which the Friedmans refer to again here, gives far more votes to those with a lot of money.

But another crucial point for Friedman was that these "public goods," for which government must be relied upon since markets cannot produce everything, must be paid for by those who use them and not by a large social majority imposing taxes on someone else, like the wealthier households.

There is no inconsistency between a free market system and the pursuit of broad social and cultural goals, or between a free market system and compassion for the less fortunate... There is all the difference in the world, however, between two kinds of assistance through government that seem superficially similar: first, 90 percent of us agreeing to impose taxes on ourselves in order to help the bottom 10 percent, and second, 80 percent voting to impose taxes on the top 10 percent to help the bottom 10 percent.[12]

This last point is worth considering. It suggests the possibility of a tyrannical majority using the political institutions of the republic to vote through taxes on some oppressed minority. We can imagine a cruel population paying for public works by taxing a persecuted ethnic group, for example. However, the possibility of a social majority deciding to more aggressively tax a minority in a society that holds *power* over them due to their resources, like an aristocracy or a concentrated capitalist class, begins to sound rather different. The issue will return later in this chapter.

The kind of government the Friedmans and Hayek would prefer is stated clearly: "a society that puts freedom first will, as a happy by-product, end up with both greater freedom and greater equality." The policies that would be pursued are sometimes called "neoliberalism," and are those Friedman later proudly pointed to as the Reagan legacy, including "slashing taxes" and "attacking government regulations." Given the Right's long-standing antagonism to labor unions (reviewed in Chapter 1), we can take it that they wouldn't be much in the picture either, and indeed all these have been major thrusts of government policy for the last forty years.

The prescription is for a return to the public policy configurations of the late nineteenth century, the "Gilded Age," an era of gigantic monopolies that the Friedmans ironically defend in *Free to Choose*: "A myth has grown up about the United States that paints the nineteenth century as the era of the robber baron, of rugged, unrestrained individualism. Heartless monopoly capitalists allegedly exploited the poor, encouraged immigration, and then fleeced the immigrants unmercifully. Wall Street is pictured as conning Main Street... The reality was very different. Immigrants kept coming."[13] Apparently, this is meant to suggest that they were attracted by the freedom of early America, although pesky historians might also point to little "push" factors like the Irish Potato Famine.

So the neoliberal "Age of Friedman" is likely to be a return to the Gilded Age of super-powerful monopolists, child laborers and an economy staggering from boom to crash, and indeed we have moved impressively in these directions over the last forty years. There are other issues to address too, including that our "having something to say" in the political world is being swamped by a torrent of money surging through the electoral and political process. Though a very old feature of our capitalist republics, it has taken on truly fantastic proportions in the neoliberal era. The Friedmans proposed a "Personal Independence Day" from government taxes, which are described as a despotic and inefficient parasitizing of our hard-earned dollars. I would suggest instead a "Co-Dependence Day," to focus on the impressive level of control corporate money has won over the state.

You Say You Bought a Revolution

The tight historical relationship between concentrated economic wealth and state power goes back very far and indeed a lot of world history makes a lot more sense when the strategies of concentrated capital are added to the picture. To explore this broad subject I'll focus on the US, which is often recognized to be an especially money-driven society, but as we'll see the principles apply widely.

The fingerprints of money are easily seen on one of the founding documents of the modern era, the United States Constitution. The definitive work on the economics of the Constitution is Charles Beard's classic *An Economic Interpretation of the Constitution*, which in detail lays out the economic interests of the delegates to the Constitutional Convention that wrote the document, and the economic patterns of the national reaction to it and its ratification. While criticized for highlighting economic interests rather than the more conventional approach to the document, which focuses on the liberal republican ideals of the founders, Beard has a sturdy response: the founders themselves focused on economic interests heavily in their own debates while writing the document.

Consider, for example, comments by James Madison—the founding father given credit for writing much of the US Constitution—in the *Federalist Papers*, the series of articles by Madison and fellow founders Thomas Jefferson and John Jay. Madison wrote about the "diversity in the faculties of men," which meant:

... the possession of different degrees and kinds of property immediately results; and from the influence of these on the sentiments and views of the respective proprietors, ensues a division of society into different interests and parties... The most common and durable source of factions has been the various and unequal distribution of property. Those who hold and those who are without property have ever formed distinct interests in society. Those who are creditors, and those who are debtors, fall under a like discrimination. A landed interest, a manufacturing interest, a mercantile interest, a moneyed interest, with many lesser interests, grow up of necessity in civilized nations and divide them into different classes, actuated by different sentiments and views.[14]

Much as with Adam Smith (see Chapter 1), figures like Madison tended to have a realistic picture of society that included class analysis.

Beard observes that the giant majority of the delegates to the Constitutional Convention in Philadelphia had large economic interests that would be affected directly by the document they shaped, including many large landowners, major merchants, slaveholding plantation owners, government bondholders, a few manufacturers and especially commercial lawyers who represented these great interests. Beard's conclusion is that a whopping five sixths of the Philadelphia delegates were "immediately, directly, and personally interested… and were to a greater or lesser extent economic beneficiaries" from the Constitution's adoption.[15]

The main economic interests of this time shaped the Constitution to stop laws that limited their wealth and power. State governments had sometimes enacted "stay laws," which prevented landlords from evicting indebted tenant farmers or kept creditors from seizing assets from penniless borrowers. State governments were declining to recognize the bonds issued to pay for the revolution's giant debts and some states issued their own paper money, devaluing existing cash and making debts easier to repay. Finally, the states were at the mercy of Great Britain's powerful Royal Navy, which frequently stole the contents of merchant ships or forced their crews to work for them instead.

The Constitution as a document almost perfectly conforms to these issues. It restricts the ability of the states to infringe on private contracts, so they cannot respond to popular demands among the electorate for debt relief; and, likewise, states are prohibited from issuing money or impinging on private property rights. The federal government, on the other hand, has its powers spread apart and separated, which Madison famously described as a "separation of powers." On the basis of the philosophy of freedom we reviewed in the Introduction, this sounds pretty good—we often think of concentrated power as being an obstacle to freedom, so if the powers of government are split up into legislative, executive and judicial branches, that would seem to aid the cause of human liberty.

Except the specifics of the plan serve more to bar the electorate from influencing the state and to maintain the status quo. Madison, who again is considered to be the father of the Constitution, wrote in his class analysis that owing to the "diversity" of people's ability to get rich and gain or inherit property, "The causes of faction cannot be removed," which meant contention in society was inevitable. This created the danger of different interests combining, and creating a faction or class organization that could overwhelm the minority of the propertied. The current system was created to preserve for Madison's class the benefits of the freedom of commerce provided by a republic, but to always limit the power of other, potentially numerically larger classes and factions. The limits on voting, and the layers between the federal government and the people, would have the effect of "passing [laws] through the medium of a chosen body of citizens." Only one part of the new federal government, the lower chamber of Congress, was democratically elected under the original Constitution. And of course, voting restrictions set by the states exempted from the voting franchise women, indentured servants in the North, slaves and those without land or a business concern. And the sheer size of the country would "make it less probable that a majority of the whole will have a common motive to invade the rights of other citizens; or if such a common motive exists, it will be more difficult for all who feel it to discover their strength and to act in unison with each other."[16]

Clarifying, Beard cites a letter Madison wrote to Jefferson about the dynamics of power and government. Among other fascinating insights, Madison baldly states "the invasion of private property is *chiefly* to be apprehended, not from acts of Government contrary to the sense of its constituents, but from acts in which the Government is the mere instrument of the major number of the constituents." All these little-remembered historical facts are a manifestation of what John Jay, the first US Supreme Court Chief Justice and coauthor of the *Federalist Papers*, memorably said: "Those who own the country ought to govern it."[17]

This tradition continues, as documented by perceptive scholars like Thomas Ferguson of the University of Massachusetts, prominent for his development of the investment theory of party competition. He describes "the 'Golden Rule' of political analysis—to discover who rules, follow the gold," meaning "trace the origins and financing of the campaign."[18] The heart of this school's argument is pretty simple—politics gets complicated, and taking time to get involved in it at some level, learning about the issues, and the effort required to fight political confrontations, are limited resources for most working people. In other words, engaging in politics is an *investment* of time and energy, and the more resources you have access to, the bigger an investment you can make. Ferguson's "core proposition" was that "the investment theory of parties holds that parties are more accurately analyzed as *blocs of major investors who coalesce to advance candidates representing their interests*."[19] The basic "money in politics" problem that folks generally see today, on the Right and Left, can be explored more carefully.

The relatively large resources required in this picture mean that the biggest political "investors" are likely to be the great business entities and wealthy families. However, Ferguson observes at the outset that "The theory does not deny the possibility that masses of voters might indeed become the major investors in an electoral system;" however, "ordinary voters require strong channels that directly facilitate mass deliberation and expression... By far the most important of such organizations, of course, are labor unions."[20]

Ferguson applies an extremely strong research process showing the model's ability to explain American history from the War of 1812 through the 1990s, observing that major public policy shifts tend to follow business maneuvering. For example, while financial interests have historically favored free trade, since it broadens their investment opportunities and encourages overall growth, the industrial sectors had perennially demanded tariffs—taxes on imported goods. This had led them to frequently take opposing sides on these and other political issues, even while sharing interests like private property rights and breaking labor unions. However, by the early 1900s "The financiers were investing more and more in American industry. They were beginning to acquire some of the same interests in tariffs, aggressive foreign policies, and export drives... With manufacturing now playing a new pivotal role in the plans of the major investors in both banks and railroads, a switch of sentiment on the tariff was inevitable."[21]

This analysis highlights the role of commerce and helps to explain the gigantic amounts of cash involved in shaping policy today. The Center for Responsive Politics is the most respected nonprofit research group, tracking elections and lobbying data, and organizing it by candidate, party, industry, or company. The totals are pretty stupefying—in the 2012 US presidential race, Obama's campaign and allied groups spent a total of over $964 million, while Romney and allies spent about $1.14 billion.[22] In the 2014 congressional race, the overall cost of campaigns for the House was $1 billion, with the Republicans leading the Democrats somewhat; in the Senate race, $608 million was spent on far fewer campaigns, with a narrower GOP edge.[23] The Republican edge in money may have been reflected in their majorities in both congressional chambers, though Romney's small edge didn't avail him.

Much of the huge increase in political spending is channeled through Super PACs, entities legalized by the now-infamous *Citizens United* Supreme Court decision, which allows corporations or unions the ability to spend unlimited amounts supporting candidates through these Political Action Committees, provided they do not officially coordinate policy.[24] Notably, the business news service Bloomberg's 2015 poll found that by large margins, Americans oppose the Citizens United decision that allowed these Super PACs — with 78 percent calling it a bad decision that ought to be overturned, and 17 percent saying it was a good decision.[25] The conservative *Wall Street Journal* confirms Ferguson's investor theory, quoting the head of a pro-Ted Cruz Super PAC who openly states: "The savviest investors — in and out of politics — demand performance metrics and accountability."[26]

Beyond the world of campaign funding, consider lobbying, the process of trying to encourage, persuade or bully political figures into taking different positions. Lobbying has become an extremely unpopular occupation, usually on the expectation that so much additional money behind one side of an argument will trump anything a regular constituent says, and given the numbers you can see why. The highest lobbying spenders for 2015 are led, unsurprisingly, by the US Chamber of Commerce, the largest of the business organizations (see Chapter 1). The Chamber spent a whopping $64 million in that year, while the National Association of Manufacturers itself spent $14 million and the Business Roundtable, another business group made up of the CEOs of the largest 100 US companies, spent $14 million also.[27] Several larger corporations also spend tens of millions individually. Notably, no labor union cracks the top twenty. The highest spending sectors of the economy were FIRE (finance, insurance, and real estate) at a towering $352 million in 2015, health services at $381 million and communications with $281 million. Labor's total for the year: $33 million.[28] This wild imbalance in access to money for political investment is one reason that Roger Martin wrote in *Harvard Business Review* that "Labor is on its own politically in the 21st century."[29]

While most political science specialists still prefer to see politics as about a debate of ideas, with decisions made by various "majoritarian" processes where all citizens and groups are represented, some researchers are more savvy. Professor of Politics Martin Gilens ran a giant mathematical analysis of nearly 2000 national surveys that classified respondents by income, finding the:

> ... impact of average citizens' "preferences" to be at "a nonsignificant, near-zero level..." Not only do ordinary citizens not have *uniquely* substantial power over policy decisions; they have little or no independent influence on policy at all... When a majority of citizens disagrees with economic elites or with organized interests, they usually lose. Moreover, because of the strong status quo bias built into the U.S. political system, even when fairly large majorities of Americans favor policy change, they generally do not get it.[30]

While the US is something of a paradise for political spending, political investment is definitively not limited to that country or the developed world. Global experience in recent times often conforms to this pattern; although always with unique political conditions. In China, the government remains authoritarian and outwardly committed to its Communist rhetoric, but since the late 1970s the country has trended toward capitalism along with the rest of the world in the neoliberal period. However, China's government is independent and strong enough to have insisted on policies that actually develop the country, from technology sharing by companies seeking market access to maintaining a cheap currency to boost exports.

But as the country's double-digit economic growth rate continued through the decades, huge private fortunes have arisen and the country has taken on more characteristics of market dominance of politics. Global CEOs are actively solicited for advice by the Chinese president, even publicly, and private investment has continued even as China's economy has recently cooled, and mobile capital allows lower value-added manufacturing to move to Indonesia and Bangladesh.[31] Indeed, China's own legislature is increasingly dominated by the country's wealthy—*The New York Times* reports that "Among the 1,271 richest Chinese people tracked by the Shanghai-based Hurun Report, a record 203, or more than one in seven, are delegates to the nation's Parliament or its advisory body."[32] Although the Congress is a rubber stamp for the ruling Party, "the concentration of wealth in its ranks reflects the growing influence of the rich in Chinese politics. This is no accident. Starting more than a decade ago, the Communist Party, founded to empower workers and peasants and quash the capitalist class, began to welcome wealthy members to broaden its appeal and buttress its authority."

The pattern continues next door in Hong Kong, the former British Imperial possession and longtime base for Western trade with China. A part of China since 1999, the local business elite has consistently sided with the mainland government's preselection of which candidates will be allowed to run for office in Hong Kong.[33] Indeed, they stage counterdemonstrations against those demanding democracy, in which *The Times* reports that

"Many participants brought along their Indonesian and Filipino domestic helpers... with some given Chinese flags to wave."

Each case is unique in its details and in many instances the right-wing view of this issue, based on "crony capitalism," is relevant. Crony capitalism describes a nominal market economy, but one with monopoly, oligopoly or other concentrated structures, because industries were put in the hands of allies or "cronies" of the state regime. A classic case is that of Carlos Slim, the Mexican billionaire, whose telecom corporations are profiled in *The Wall Street Journal*: "His Telefonos de Mexico SAB and its cellphone affiliate Telcel have 92% of all fixed-lines and 73% of all cellphones. As Mr. Rockefeller did before him, Mr. Slim has accumulated so much power that he is considered untouchable in his native land, a force as great as the state itself."[34]

The Age of Friedman has changed Mexico:

Monopolies have long been a feature of Mexico's economy. But in the past, politicians acted as a brake on big business to ensure that the business class didn't threaten their power. But political control faded in the 1990s with the privatization of much of the economy... Congress routinely kills legislation that threatens his interests, and his firms account for a chunk of the nation's advertising revenue, making the media reluctant to criticize him.

The New York Times also wrote that "Mr. Slim's style of wealth accumulation is not rare in modern Mexico. From television to tortillas, vast swaths of the Mexican economy are controlled by monopolies or oligopolies. Many of Mexico's billionaires were created by the government during the privatization of state-owned companies in the 1990s."[35]

However, the inevitable usage of the quite legitimate "crony capitalism" concept is as an opportunistic tool to keep focus off the power of money and market share. As Chapter 1 explores extensively, all historical evidence shows that capital concentrates with economic growth and monopolies arise in free-market settings, quite consistently. The pre-regulation and pre-progressive taxation era of the Gilded Age shows pure capitalism clearly, and its gigantic nationwide monopolies far from an era of freedom from the ravages of power. So in many markets, the oligopoly or monopoly may indeed arise directly from government privatization that places an existing state monopoly in the hands of a crony of the regime, as in the case of the billionaire Slim or the Russian "oligarchy" of post-Soviet monopolists. But at least as often, markets get to their towering heights of monopoly all on their own—indeed, Slim himself, while clearly a giant beneficiary of shady government asset sales in the "crony" model, was born wealthy and held a good deal of cash at the right moment, when Mexico's phone system was privatized in the 1980s at the beginning of the Age of Friedman.[36] He has since played an aggressive monopoly game, cornering markets and crushing competitors within the marketplace. The *Journal* refers in passing to Rockefeller's "stranglehold on refining oil" as a parallel to Slim—a free-market monopoly for anyone willing to open their eyes.

These general instances are illustrative, but the investment perspective shows its mettle best in Ferguson's analysis of the rise of the New Deal in capitalist America. The New Deal was the program for economic recovery during the endless and grinding conditions of the Great Depression of the 1930s. The series of major policy changes dating from that time includes the creation of Social Security, the public pension system for the elderly and disabled; the National Labor Relations Act, which essentially legalized unions and the legitimacy of collective bargaining for workers; the establishment of a national minimum wage, setting a floor under worker earnings; the Glass-Steagall Act, which broke off risky investment banking from the commercial banking field that held Americans' deposits; deficit-spending employment programs and other progressive social policies. The rise of those social policies—which are extremely popular—and eventually their decline, are all driven by decisions and strategic maneuvers of coalitions of political investors in shifting economic conditions.

Ferguson observed that at the end of World War I, Wall Street split from industry over the issues of the tariff. Meanwhile, labor unions had been almost totally crushed before World War I and were crushed again after the war. But in the Depression, labor roared back to life amid "epic class conflicts" and in time became a significant political actor.[37] While some employers reacted with the usual aggressive tactics, some firms that were relatively capital-intensive rather than labor-intensive were prepared to accept labor unions among their smaller, more professional workforces. In the 1930s, the more capital-intensive corporations and the free-trade-oriented Wall Street banks were prepared to form an alliance, in which organized labor with its own resources could participate as a political investor. This new matrix made up the New Deal coalition: "World War I disrupted these cozy relations between American industry and finance... while none of them were pro-union they preferred to conciliate rather than to repress their workforce."[38] Ferguson's point is that the unusual combination of gigantic corporations and successful unions can be understood with an investment-based analysis.

But most investor coalitions, just like political ones, can break apart and change shape as the broader economy and society evolve, and indeed the programs of the New Deal have been in pronounced decline since the late 1970s, along with parallel programs around the world. This trend has dominated the Age of Friedman and its neoliberal policy, itself arising from shifting investors as well as the failure of the New Deal to take radical steps, like removing the tremendous economic power of concentrated rich classes and their companies.

The New Deal, Dealt

The New Deal and other public programs of the era, like the Great Society measures of the 1960s such as Medicare and Medicaid, and the environmental legislation of the 1970s, meant that rich families and their large corporations faced far higher tax rates, confronted significantly tighter regulations on their businesses, had their monopoly-making mergers blocked and mostly had to accept the legal existence of labor unions. But the rich and their corporate property kept their *power*, through retaining diminished but still potent concentrated fortunes and market shares. This meant that the New Deal, despite rhetoric from some of its supporters and opponents alike, was no break from capitalism. This limited reform-based approach contained the seeds of its own destruction, for by leaving the power of wealth and big business alive, these opponents of New Deal programs could work against them, and over decades have successfully restored many of the old conditions of the Gilded Age in our neoliberal era.

During the New Deal, American business partially accepted expanded government and labor organization, but also bided its time under the postwar liberal period, maintaining more friendly ideas in circulation until conditions could be shifted in their favor. New York University history professor Kim Phillips-Fein's *Invisible Hands* does an impeccable job telling the story, following influential businessmen of the period, for example at GE. General Electric came into existence as a free-market monopoly, "Morganized" from several merged appliance firms by Wall Street titan J.P. Morgan (see Chapter 1). GE was among those global market-leading, capital-heavy corporations that was willing to accommodate its relatively small labor force when it demanded union recognition and ultimately supported the New Deal.

However, the great strike wave that followed World War II

shook GE's management, especially the 1946 electrician's strike, as Phillips-Fein describes: "In some of the striking communities, for much of the strike, the workers essentially controlled access to the plants. Hundreds of workers encircled the factories in long picket lines, refusing access to white-collar and management employees and allowing only limited numbers of maintenance men through the lines."[39] This kind of strike action is related to union tactics like plant occupation or "sit-down strikes," where a community-supported labor force takes control of the capital they work with, and tends to be far more alarming to firms like GE, many of which turned from being New Deal advocates to avowed opponents. Certainly the corporate organizations of the time, like the big-industry National Association of Manufacturers, remained strongly opposed.

This was immediately indicated by labor legislation, which even in this era of relative union strength put several basic union tools outside the law. In the immediate aftermath of the postwar strike wave, Congress overrode Truman's veto in passing the Taft-Hartley Act, which outlawed sympathy strikes (strike action taken by one union to support unions in another), mandated that supervisors and foremen be kept out of shop bargaining units, and other union-weakening policies. The National Labor Relations Board, created to adjudicate union elections, itself ruled under the Eisenhower administration that "employers had the right to hold 'captive audience' meetings during working hours, at which managers could try to persuade workers not to vote for a union; in the past, employers had been obliged to provide union organizers with equal time to speak to employees."[40]

The corporate world itself separately developed new methods, many of them part of the so-called "Mohawk Valley Formula," named for the location of a failed strike against Remington Rand. Elements of the formula include the traditional threat of violence and stockpiling of weapons by the company, but rather than outright violence newer techniques were used, like insulting labor organizers as disloyal, or threatening to close or move if the union wins, and especially setting up groups of workers sympathetic to the company to publicly oppose the union, but without revealing the role of the company as the funder. These dirty corporate playbooks drove the course of the US labor movement's "union density," the proportion of its workforce organized into a collective bargaining unit. It peaked in 1954 at 33.5 percent and has declined ever since.[41]

But less appreciated among the main tools of the business world to undermine unions and the New Deal was the cultivation of intellectuals. Intellectuals and academics who considered wealth not to be a source of power, but willing instead to oppose the power of unions and government programs, found themselves receiving significant support. Their work would encourage skeptical Americans and Europeans to forget their suspicion of concentrated wealth and see power only in its enemies. One important figure in this use of conservative intellectuals by business was Harold Luhnow, a Kansas City businessman. His company's well-endowed philanthropic trust, the Volker Fund, fully funded Friedrich Hayek's salary over his ten-year tenure at the University of Chicago. The Mont Perelin society, the preeminent libertarian think tank, had its academic participants' travel costs paid by the Fund and Milton Friedman's book *Capitalism and Freedom*, which this book is a response to, was based on lectures by Friedman it had sponsored.[42]

This history is painfully ironic, considering that Friedman himself argued that New Deal programs like Social Security arose because liberal intellectuals propagandized the public into supporting them, manipulating people into getting behind Big Government. But in reality, a huge grassroots movement during the Great Depression, when millions were robbed of their own security in the market, was the origin of the program.[43] If Friedman wanted to see a social movement driven by intellectuals with a hidden personal motivation, he could have looked at his own neoliberal campaign. As Phillips-Fein summarizes, "It is not clear that the romantic, political free-market approach of the Mont Perelin Society would have survived without the support of businessmen."[44]

But crucially, the essential support from business was kept quiet, to obscure the social elements these intellectuals worked for. Hayek wrote to Luhnow that:

> ... any effort in the sphere of ideas, if it is to be effective, must avoid even the appearance of being dependent on any material interests, and for that reason we have been careful not to include in the list of persons originally invited, anyone, however sympathetic with our aims, who might be thought by the public to represent specific interests.

In fact, the record shows that across the most conservative institutions created in this period, from the right-wing *National Review* magazine to the American Enterprise Institute to the Mont Perelin Society, "All of these organizations relied on the contributions of businessmen," often secretly.[45] The Heritage Foundation was created with money from the right-wing Coors beer family, while the energy industry's Koch brothers proudly founded the arch-libertarian Cato Institute (originally the Charles Koch Foundation).

This business community strategy of fighting on all fronts—government, business investments, media and building an intellectual rationale—was explicitly thought out in a particularly important but almost unknown document, the "Powell memo." The 1971 document, actually titled "Attack on American Free Enterprise System," was written by Lewis Powell, a prominent attorney, for his friend Eugene Sydnor, the head of the Education Committee for the US Chamber of Commerce. Powell suggested in the memo, marked "Confidential" but later leaked, that the pressures on business in the early 1970s had become too great to tolerate, and business would have to use its resources to organize and fight back.[46] Because so many of its proposals came to pass, and since it represents an insider view of corporate organization and political planning, it deserves to be quoted at length.

Powell began "No thoughtful person can question that the American economic system is under broad attack," but insisted "We are not dealing with sporadic or isolated attacks from a relatively few extremists or even from the minority socialist cadre. Rather, the assault on the enterprise system is broadly based..." After praising the work of Friedman, Powell condemns "economic illiteracy," adding "This setting of the 'rich' against the 'poor,' of business against the people, is the cheapest and most dangerous kind of politics." Powell ought to have consulted Madison, Smith or Martin Luther King about faction and class conflict.

Based on this survey of the situation, Powell's core message was "the time has come... for the wisdom, ingenuity and resources of American business to be marshalled against those who would destroy it... This involves far more than an increased emphasis on 'public relations' or 'governmental affairs'—two areas in which corporations have long invested substantial sums." Turning to the "Possible Role of the Chamber of Commerce," Powell explicitly backed up the arguments reviewed in Chapter 1 about business organizing trade bodies, while ruthlessly fighting worker organization. "Strength lies in organization, in careful long-range planning and implementation, in consistency of action over an indefinite period of years, and in the political power available only through united action and national organizations."

Focusing on the college campuses as "the single most dynamic source" of opposition to capitalism, Powell not only attributes this in part to the freewheeling inquiry required on campus, but also suggests that faculty who "are unsympathetic to the enterprise system... are often personally attractive and magnetic; they are stimulating teachers, and their controversy attracts student following; they are prolific writers and lecturers; they author many of the textbooks, and they exert enormous influence." The attractive and magnetic part is very, very true. But Powell has a trump card: the people actually in charge of colleges are sympathetic. "The boards of trustees of our universities overwhelmingly are composed of men and women who are leaders in the system."

Asking "What Can Be Done About the Public?" Powell suggests "The national television networks should be monitored in the same way that textbooks should be kept under constant surveillance." He continues,

"The average member of the public thinks of 'business' as an impersonal corporate entity, owned by the very rich and managed by over-paid executives... It is time for American business—which has demonstrated the greatest capacity in all history to produce and to influence consumer decisions— to apply their talents vigorously to the preservation of the system itself."

Politically, Powell is consistent: "There should not be the slightest hesitation to press vigorously in all political arenas for support of the enterprise system. Nor should there be reluctance to penalize politically those who oppose it." But most relevant for the subject of this book are Powell's comments on the system's "Relationship to Freedom... The threat to the free enterprise system is not merely a matter of economics. It is also a threat to individual freedom... the only alternatives to free enterprise are varying degrees of bureaucratic regulation of individual freedom." The common claim that "there is no alternative" to capitalism, except a loss of freedom, will be explored in Chapter 5.

Weeks after preparing the memo for the Chamber, Powell

was appointed to the US Supreme Court. But even as he wrote, the political turning point approached. The major strategic pivot of the corporate world and elite families away from the postwar "liberal consensus" of the New Deal era occurred in the mid- to late-seventies, when inflation reached high levels and corporate profitability fell. The rising prices reflected a long list of social forces, but labor unions' wage-increasing strikes were blamed and demonization of them rose in media. At the same time, industrial profitability fell with the recovery of the industrial economies of Japan and German-centered Europe after World War II, which meant more competition for global sales. Combined with the labor antagonism and what *Businessweek* called "America's Growing Antibusiness Mood," the business world decisively shifted from grudging New Deal acceptance and labor accommodation, to pursuing the goals of the Powell memo.[47] Beside a new emphasis on global production and world capital mobility, it meant support for neoliberal policy.

President Reagan entered office after a campaign aggressively funded by the corporate world to bring labor, inflation and government social programs into line. A *Wall Street Journal* survey reported a whopping 87 percent of the CEOs of big corporations supported Reagan, a significantly higher rate of support than he received from small firms.[48] And no wonder, for the neoliberal economic policies of his conservative administration were based directly on the work of those intellectuals that business had supported with their rich resources for years. Reagan's staff handed out a 1000-page Heritage Foundation policy program to his Cabinet in its first meeting, he spoke at AEI conventions and while speaking at a conservative political dinner, "He made special mention of his gratitude to Friedrich von Hayek, Milton Friedman, and Ludwig von Mises... for their intellectual acuity in dark times," as Phillips-Fein recounts.[49]

Implementing these policies in the "Age of Friedman" that followed the Reagan revolution has taken different forms — from deregulation to the inequality-boosting tax cuts referred to in Chapter 1. As social programs were cut back globally, the term "austerity" came into increasing use to describe the lowered levels of social supports and public goods that government could provide.

Some effects of austerity are simple, like the cutbacks on social safety net programs like food stamps. As Reagan's tax cuts for the richest households and their corporations created huge budget deficits, budgets got balanced not by retaxing the rich, or cutting the military spending we use to overthrow pesky foreign governments, but by cutting social supports. When the US Congress cut the food stamp program by $5 billion, a modest amount by national standards, it meant a reduction in the monthly total received to terribly low amounts, a big deal considering that one in seven Americans used the program at the time and almost half of recipients were children.[50] The effects damage poor neighborhoods as well, since with less money to spend, stamp recipients buy less from local stores, a ripple effect in the economy sometimes called the "multiplier." Much like when a major employer closes and other businesses feel the echo in the lower spending by laid-off workers that follows, business or government investments tend to have "knock-on" effects that magnify the impacts of their decisions.

The clearest place to see this is in health. Public Health expert David Stuckler and Professor of Medicine Sanjay Basu document the ramifications of austerity in public health programs in their outstanding book *The Body Economic*. Among their careful data analysis is a comparison of health outcomes in Iceland and Greece. When Iceland's banks went bankrupt in the world financial crisis of 2008, the IMF stuck to the neoliberal script and was willing to extend emergency loans only on terms of extreme austerity—Iceland's public spending was to be cut by a dramatic 15 percent of GDP, in order to afford payments to the banks' creditors equal to *half* of Iceland's gross income for several

years.[51] Almost unbelievably, the IMF designated healthcare a "luxury good," but Iceland's government put it to a vote. In a 2010 referendum the people of Iceland voted 93 percent against the IMF austerity program to pay off the international creditors of the banks' risky investments.[52]

Iceland did the opposite of economists' demands:

By first rejecting the IMF's plan for radical austerity, it protected a modern-day equivalent of the New Deal... In 2007, Iceland's government spending as a fraction of GDP was 42.3 percent. This increased to 57.7 percent in 2008... This increase didn't lead to inflation, runaway debt that has been impossible to pay back, or foreign dependency—the predicted disasters that austerity advocates claim will result from stimulus programs.

Iceland expanded social support programs of public housing, job retention and debt relief for small businesses, and its health spending rose, to a quarter of GDP in 2009.[53]

The success story of Iceland's rejection of austerity is contrasted by Stuckler and Basu with the tragedy of Greece at the same time. In Greece, an even more drastic IMF bailout was offered, but unlike in Iceland, the birthplace of democracy canceled a planned public referendum on austerity. The cuts were heinous: the IMF demanded that public health spending drop to 6 percent of GDP to free up budget money to repay foreign banks and lenders, while governments supporting the IMF, like Germany, typically spend around 10 percent of GDP on health.[54] In a horrifying plunge, Greece went from a lower-rung developed country to health conditions more common in the developing world, with OECD data showing a 40 percent spike in infant mortality and an almost 50 percent jump in unmet healthcare needs. Indeed, "The Health Ministry continued to avoid collecting and publicly disclosing many standard health statistics."[55]

Crucially, with Greece forced into austerity after passing on democracy, it did not start getting out of debt. In fact, as its economy slowed and tilted into recession under austerity, its debt-to-GDP ratio *rose*. This lead the IMF to actually assign its economists to recalculate its assumed multiplier values, finding a value higher than one, meaning that spending can stimulate the economy, in line with the Icelandic experience.[56]

This austerity applies worldwide, as global financial institutions like the IMF still put health spending on the chopping block as soon as a country requires a bailout after some dictator loots its assets. The legacy of this aggressive budget balancing at the expense of the poor countries can blow back on the rest of the world—many observers noted that the World Health Organization, a UN body, was slow in its response to the 2014 Ebola outbreak in western Africa. *The New York Times* reported that "The W.H.O... has been badly weakened by budget cuts in recent years, hobbling its ability to respond in parts of the world that need it most... The disease spread for months before being detected because much of the work of spotting outbreaks was left to desperately poor countries ill prepared for the task."[57] The WHO was able to manage large health crises like SARS in China, Ebola in the Congo and plague in India, but then "the global financial crisis struck. The W.H.O. had to cut nearly \$1 billion from its proposed two-year budget, which today stands at \$3.98 billion... The whims of donors also greatly influenced the W.H.O.'s agenda, with gifts, often to advance individual causes, far surpassing dues from member nations." More alarmingly, the WHO's "epidemic and pandemic response department" was dissolved and its components spread to other WHO bodies. Austerity plainly contributed to the Ebola epidemic, which killed thousands and terrified the world.

With austerity in health and education causing such painfu direct and side-effect costs, where else can government turn fix the budget hole created by the waves of upper-income

cuts? A 2014 public poll by the Harris agency found that it can be hard to decide—their report was titled "What to Cut when Majorities of Americans Support Most Major Government Services?" They found over 75 percent of the public supported Medicaid, environmental protection and defense, and over 85 percent supported social security, crime fighting and Medicare.[58] Harris also found that support for these programs has increased slightly over the last few years. This pattern of support for safety nets and public goods programs associated with the New Deal period is common globally, but all these programs (except defense) are aggressively targeted for further austerity, before and after the rise of Trump.

Shadow Puppets

Today's money-centered, neoliberal world offers endless further examples of the power of wealthy social elements and concentrated markets to shape political events, from Europe to Asia to Latin America. The history of this phenomenon in the developing world will make up the next section. But for now, the incredibly thorough degree of control of capital in affairs of state, and the contrary fact that it is still not all-powerful, should be explored. And for an emblematic case, the US is still the ideal test setting, famous globally for its limited and declining controls on how cash shapes politics. Recent years have shown the US House of Representatives, the lower chamber of the American legislature, to be a particularly gross showcase.

Consider the Boehner resignation. House Speaker John Boehner resigned his position after being the face of the congressional Republicans' aggressive efforts to undo Obamacare, the 2013 government shutdown and demands for aggressive spending cuts.[59] But while there was much discussion of the political maneuvering, as usual little attention went to the crucial and shifting role of corporate America, to whom the GOP owes its congressional majorities. The surprising events leading to the Ayn Rand-reading "moderate" Paul Ryan becoming Speaker reveals the degree to which the US Congress is a ruling-class plaything.

The Tea Party was founded by Koch brother money and Fox News free publicity—the conservative *Wall Street Journal* reported that "Business groups spent millions of dollars on the [2010] mid-term elections to help secure a GOP majority in Congress," while the more liberal *Washington Post*'s rendering was "business groups have helped Boehner and his counterparts in the Senate raise millions of dollars to put Republicans in office, including the 2010 election of tea party lawmakers who have now roiled the GOP."[60] Since its origin, the Tea Party's backers hoped to use an aggressive, talk-radio fed constituency and rowdy House members as momentum to continue the long project of overturning the remains of the New Deal and Great Society programs—progressive taxation on the rich, Social Security, Medicare and industrial regulation.[61]

But it's not easy being a political puppeteer—business thought it could control the Tea Party, but it turned out it can't. The *Journal* observes that "the rebellious wing" of the Party has refused to carry out even basic legislative functions, which meant that not only were the New Deal programs and tax levels under the ax, but also "the top legislative priorities of large American companies were thrown into deeper disarray."[62] This was not the plan. Increasingly rabid GOP primary elections, fed by paranoid right-wing media, usually happen prior to the giant corporate funding that seals the deal in the general elections. This resulted in a growing "Freedom Caucus"—the current Tea Party-derived wing of GOP representatives. While this wing is archconservative, its "anti-elitism" has run up against business priorities, in a way corporate mega-donors hadn't expected.

Beside a willingness to flirt repeatedly with government shutdowns and even debt defaults, which horrify businesses and most especially Wall Street, the caucus' free-market ideology led to business defeats like defunding the Export-Import Bank. The Bank extends credit to foreign purchasers of US-made products and services, serving to boost exports and corporate sales. Corporate America doesn't take such misbehavior lying down, no more from Republicans it paid to elect than from Democrats it also paid to elect. In a political system where lobbyists openly refer to "investing in" candidates and having "buyer's remorse" when they sometimes disobey, resources will be put into action.[63]

And so it was that in Alabama in October 2013, the Chamber and other business firms started spending to *defeat* Tea Party candidates, after having spent so much to create and install them.[64] In a special primary runoff pitting a Chamber-backed business candidate against a shutdown-supporting incumbent, the Chamber's "post-government-shutdown effort to derail Tea Party candidates" kicked into high gear. Giant corporations like Caterpillar, Pfizer, BASF and AT&T, along with large industry groups like the National Retail Federation (which includes Walmart), all essentially conceded they made a mistake with the 2010 crop and pushed back toward more traditional pro-corporate conservatism.

The US Chamber decided on which candidates to support in part on whether they voted to end the shutdown.[65] Corporate America succeeded in some House races and failed in others, as business funding competed with the extreme "libertarian ideology" a Chamber sympathizer complained of, along with the fact that "extreme conservatives tend to be more reliable voters," as *The New York Times* suggested.[66] This mixed record isn't expected to deter the Chamber and other business groups — as *Bloomberg Businessweek* reported, "The chamber's goal is to send a message to House Republicans that those who oppose its agenda will face political consequences."[67]

All this meant that the 2014 "midterm elections were billed as a resurrection of sorts for the party establishment after the

Chamber of Commerce and other groups, aligned with the business wing of the party, repelled conservative challenges," as *The Wall Street Journal* put it. The Chamber spent $50 million, a gigantic amount for a congressional election year.[68] This especially visible control of the republic by money was a major contributor to the unpredictable campaigns of 2016, including the Sanders and Trump campaigns.

Through this whole period of major swings in the political investments of the business world, Speaker Boehner "was seen by many in the business community as a bulwark against tea-party excesses," as the business press put it. So the Speaker's departure, lamented by hugely powerful business groups like the US Chamber of Commerce and the National Association of Manufacturers, threw a wrench into elite efforts to control the Republic.[69] For while Boehner's replacement was the extreme anti-New Deal but pro-stability Congressman Paul Ryan, business media like the *Journal* watched apprehensively the growing list of giant demands made by the Freedom Caucus. It included numerous "policy promises" from the Speaker, but most interesting from the point of view of business control, Speaker candidate Kevin McCarthy before his withdrawal "pledged to defend any GOP incumbent against possible campaign attacks from outside groups, including the U.S. Chamber of Commerce."[70]

Government shutdowns are becoming part of the Tea Party era of US governance and arise each time a new funding bill or a debt-ceiling increase are needed. Shutdowns are treated as theater by the extreme GOP, with buffoons like Senator Ted Cruz playing to TV audiences as standing on anti-government principle. But shutdowns are enormously disruptive and expensive, and threats to allow a default on public debt are far worse—Fox News viewers are often unaware that US government bonds, which the Treasury Department issues to borrow money, are the cornerstone of the national and indeed global financial systems, owing to their historically negligible risk of default. But in the 2013 shutdown, the rating agency Fitch put US bonds on "rating watch negative," meaning they might be downgraded from their impeccable AAA status.[71] Another main agency, Standard & Poor's, actually downgraded US debt to AA after the 2011 crisis. These dramatic steps sent waves through the system, as the millions of transactions based on the bonds and related instruments abruptly seemed less safe. The broader effect is to inject new uncertainty into an already jittery global marketplace. For this reason, *The New York Times* described "fear" on Wall Street of another disruptive shutdown, while *The Wall Street Journal* reported that the 2013 shutdown "cut between two-tenths and six-tenths of a percentage point from real GDP in that year's fourth quarter, according to government and private estimates."[72]

Ryan has a 93-percent legislation rating from the US Chamber, which heartily approved his 2015 budget proposal, which would have made over a trillion dollars in cuts from welfare, food stamps and other safety net programs, cut other domestic programs by a half-trillion dollars, repealed the Affordable Care Act and created a special "emergency" war fund to shield the Pentagon from spending caps.[73] But Ryan's history of advocating immigration reform still put him under a cloud with Freedom Caucus, which couldn't bring 80 percent of its membership to agree to vote for him.[74]

The 2016 election, dominated by the elevation to power of idiot racist TV ham Donald Trump, is a reaction against this reign of campaign cash, even while the *Journal* reported that "Corporations Bet on GOP Senate Control," as "corporate PACs plowed $3 million into the campaigns of Republican candidates... 15 times as much as they contributed to Democrats in those same races... Corporations generally split their PAC money fairly evenly between Republicans and Democrats, with a slight majority of donations going to the side that is winning."[75] So while "Corporations are extremely cautious in how they dole out campaign funds," in the most competitive Senate races Corporate America made bolder moves, as "business PACs directed 99% of their donations to the Republican candidate."

But while the Chamber leans heavily Republican in recent races, there was a major exception in 2016 as the CRP reports the US Chamber gave $13,865 to Clinton's campaign, while a pitiful $520 is recorded as being donated to Trump.[76] This of course reflects the highly unconventional Republican candidate and Clinton's own conservative, pro-business record, despite New Deal affectations during the primary to fend off Senator Sanders. But with Clinton's loss we must confront the question of how the Chamber was thwarted in this staggering race, a question debated with an enormous level of passion and rather little evidence-based argument.

To see how this episode is a harbinger of rage at globalization and the deepening inequality seen in the current neoliberal period of global economic policy, consider the surprising Brexit vote, in which the areas of the UK voting most strongly for withdrawing from the European Union were those most hurt by aggressive austerity cuts to social supports under David Cameron's Conservative government.[77] Indeed, the correlation of Vote Leave turnout and fiscal cuts to satisfy austerity budget-tightening appears to be consistent even down to the ward level within UK cities. "Leave" voters' anger at their economic decline, plus a very real racist resentment of East European EU citizens' increasing immigration, led them to lash out by choosing the kick-the-Establishment-in-the-balls option, even though that is likely to make their predicament significantly worse. As will the Trump administration, for reasons reviewed below.

Perhaps fittingly, longtime rebellious writers on the political Left have most clearly resolved this, like Ajay Singh Chaudhary, who compared American voters to those in Germany, where voters "have an actual Left to flee to."[78] The great socialist writer Mike Davis captured the mood among marooned blue-collar towns (and the evangelicals who stuck with a serial divorcee and sex-assaulting candidate), which "wanted change in Washington at any price, even if it meant putting a suicide bomber in the White House."[79] Labor scholar and former TransAfrica Forum president Bill Fletcher usefully observes that Trump ran on opposition to globalization and immigration, rather than the broader neoliberal program of deregulation and tax cuts, which Trump indeed celebrated.[80]

The press was reporting Clinton's cash edge throughout 2016, even toward the end when Clinton's Super PAC had three times as much cash on hand as Trump's, which indeed held only about a third of what previous GOP nominee Mitt Romney had on hand at the same time in 2012.[81] But a detailed review suggests how Trump was able to cope with significantly less campaign cash than Clinton's team. Using the CRP data, we can confirm Clinton's major fundraising superiority, with a total of over $687 million raised, relative to Trump's $307 million.[82]

Digging into the Center's expenditures data for the White House campaigns, a major discrepancy emerges. Clinton spent just under half her campaign and PAC budgets on media—48.9 percent of the campaign total, coming to a giant $125 million.[83] But Trump's campaign spent only 37.8 percent of its budget, $30.4 million, on media.[84] And yet who would argue that Trump was under-featured on US media during the campaign? The difference is made up of "earned" media, the bizarre political term for coverage of a candidate generated by independent media sources, like an article or TV segment covering the candidacy, but without the campaign purchasing it.

This earned media is no small thing—Trump's continuous coverage was worth over $2 billion by media firm estimates.[85] The value of earned TV and radio time is usually larger than what a candidate spends on air time, but Trump's gigantic media exposure left him with two and half times the earned media value Clinton had. That goes a long way toward making up for

Trump's lower cash-on-hand and aids the money-driven politics thesis somewhat: while Trump had less money, he clearly had other material resources, in this case, his preexisting TV celebrity and ability to outrageous statement his way onto cable TV on an hourly basis. Indeed, as the world fears its uncertain future coping with the Trump administration, it could be said that being a born-rich billionaire with a reality TV persona, Trump is a definitively capitalist figure.

These ugly stories speak to the liabilities of an investment-based electoral system. But as bad as it looks within the developed world, the Third World story is the more revealing one, as far as the value of human life in the eyes of concentrated capital.

Touché Pinochet

This chapter is focused on political freedom, which Friedman said arises from the economic freedom of the market. To test this, it's important to consider the record of the developed countries' dealings with the large majority of the world's peoples, who live in the developing world. These dramatically diverse societies, which make up most of the "Global South" geographically and often still referred to as the Third World, have little in common except being subject to half a millennium of global control and colonialism by the "West" — primarily Western Europe, later joined by the US and Japan. Far beyond the standard conquering and occupying that are mainstays of human history, these were worldwide systems of control treating subject countries as sources for resource extraction, as captive markets that had to buy imported goods from the colonial power and as chess pieces in the competition among the Western imperial powers.

Recognition of this history in the Western world is low, outside of experts and political radicals, but the documentary record is extensive. Globally prominent scientist and social critic Noam Chomsky observed in his book *Year 501* that the year 1992:

... brings to an end the 500th year of the Old World Order, sometimes called the Colombian era of world history... The major theme of this Old World Order was a confrontation between the conquerors and the conquered on a global scale. It has taken various forms, and been given different names: imperialism, neocolonialism... Or, more simply, Europe's conquest of the world. By the term "Europe," we include the European-settled colonies, one of which now leads the crusade... Japan was one of the few parts of the South to escape conquest and, perhaps, not coincidentally, to join the core, with some of its former colonies in its wake.[86]

This 500-year period saw great imperial powers like Britain, France, Spain, Portugal, Holland, Italy, Belgium and Germany, outright invade or sometimes swindle local and regional powers around the globe. The imperialists came with advanced technology of violence and great ruthlessness. But they also relied on extensive claims of fine intentions, to uplift and enlighten the backward and inferior natives—much like today's neoliberal capitalism, colonialism didn't come without valuable intellectual support. Russia and the US had similarly violent and expansionist policies, but mostly without needing to cross oceans to express them. Anyone glancing at a world map from this era will observe almost the entirety of the Earth's dry land colored one of the shades of European empire.

The Old World Order became the new around the late nineteenth century, as the US industrialized during the Civil War and Gilded Age, becoming the world's biggest economy and eventually its dominant military power. Rather than outright annexing countries into a directly run empire as the Europeans did, the methods to dominate shifted to heavy investments—buying up the capital and land and productive assets of a country, and overthrowing governments if they went against foreign, or indeed domestic elites' ownership of large-scale private property. Europe shifted to this new configuration of exploitation only after World War II.

In Latin America the US business world overtook the UK in investments and share of trade during the 1920s, buying up larger shares of these lands' capital and productive wealth, and gaining the power to increasingly dominate poor foreign lands, after being previously looted by the European colonialists. "Venezuelan oil under the Gomez dictatorship, mines in Bolivia, Chile and elsewhere, and the riches of Cuba were among the favored targets... US dominance of the Brazilian market peaked after World War II, when the US supplied half of Brazil's imports and bought over 40 percent of its exports," Chomsky summarizes.[87] This was an era when the historian of the CIA, Gerald Haines, wrote "Following World War II the United States assumed, out of self-interest, responsibility for the welfare of the world capitalist system." The US pursued "neocolonial, neomercantilist policy," where territory is economically exploited to the stronger power's interest.[88]

Turning to the Middle East, a region long-recognized as especially important for its still-unparalleled energy reserves, the pattern of world power is especially clear. The champion Middle East reporter Robert Fisk's enormous book *The Great War for Civilization* is a masterwork on the region's history and for a citizen of the Western world it's not easy reading. Britain, for example, created Iraq in 1920 from provinces of the defeated Ottoman Empire, while France created Syria and Lebanon the same year.[89] The British had previously promised independence to the Arabs for helping drive out the Ottoman Turks, so when it went back on its word the Royal Air Force had to bomb rebellious tribes and the army put down large uprisings, in many of the same places the US and UK would return to a century later in the Iraq War. The British installed a puppet king, subject to an alleged referendum by the Iraqi people, which "gave him a laughably impossible 96 per cent of the vote."[90] After World

War II, the US eclipsed European power in the Middle East as it did around the world and as the European empires fell apart America often stepped in, but usually with the same policy of installing strongmen and supporting friendly regimes, including oil-rich Saudi Arabia and the other theocratic monarchies of the Persian Gulf. This isn't exactly a freedom-promoting policy.

Besides defending the horrifyingly brutal human rights records of these countries, the US and the West sold them giant volumes of weapons, from jets to ships to bombs to tanks. These sales ran into the billions even as the Arab on the street in these countries lived in poverty, sometimes with a modest state stipend for stability's sake.[91] The Saudis, like freedom-stomping potentates around the world, definitely had the money to buy arms, as did Saddam Hussein, who before becoming America's public enemy number one in 1990 was a valued US ally against the Iranians, who themselves had been a democracy before being overthrown by the US and the UK to install a dictator in 1953.

In fact, throughout the 1980s and early nineties Saddam was an especially important US ally and weapons client, and at the time of his worst atrocities. Fisk records the Iran-Iraq War: "The United States had been furnishing Iraq with satellite imagery of the Iranian battle lines since the first days of the war, and a steady stream of unofficial U.S. 'advisers' had been visiting Baghdad ever since."[92] The aid continued, even as cyanide gas was used against the Kurds in the city of Halabja. In 2002 and 2003, the Bush administration and Tony Blair's government relentlessly referred to this atrocity to justify the US invasion of Iraq; the pivotal American role was conspicuously absent from the story.

And crucially, at the same time as it was guiding and arming Iraq, the Reagan administration was sending weapons and money to the Mujahideen forces fighting the Russians, who had invaded Afghanistan.[93] Many of these fighters—including Osama bin Laden himself—would later turn their rage against the West and especially the US. Journalist Patrick Cockburn, famous for his cutting-edge reporting on the region and especially the rise of ISIS, observed:

> ... within hours of the 9/11 attacks... Washington made it clear that the anti-terror war would be waged without any confrontation with Saudi Arabia or Pakistan, two close US allies, despite the fact that without the involvement of these two countries 9/11 was unlikely to have happened. Of the nineteen hijackers that day, fifteen were Saudi. Bin Laden came from the Saudi elite. Subsequent US official documents stress repeatedly that financing for al-Qaeda and jihadi groups came from Saudi Arabia and the Gulf monarchies.[94]

But the Saudi role is doubly important:

> Saudi Arabia is influential because its oil and vast wealth make it powerful... Another factor is its propagating of Wahhabism, the fundamentalist, eighteenth-century version of Islam that imposes sharia law, relegates women to the status of second-class citizens... Wahhabism is taking over mainstream Sunni Islam. In one country after another Saudi Arabia is putting up the money for the training of preachers and the building of mosques. A result of this is the spread of sectarian strife between Sunni and Shia.[95]

Karen Armstrong comments on Saudi Arabia's "funding the building of mosques with Wahhabi preachers and establishing madrasas that provided free education to the poor. Thus, to the intense dismay of many in the Muslim world, an entire generation has grown up with this maverick form of Islam."[96]

This powermongering history continues to torment the region, with the Iraqi and Syrian Civil Wars being the most dramatic and cruel manifestations. While the West's main concerns in the conflict only arose once its horrifying collateral damage drove millions of refugees into developed Europe, the complex war has deep roots in the history of colonialism there. Journalist Charles Glass' fine history of the conflict, *Syria Burning*, observes that the rebels fighting the cruel dictatorship of Bashar al-Assad use "weapons made in America, bought by Saudi Arabia and funneled through Turkey."[97]

The Islamic State itself, Cockburn observes in his widely cited and reliable analysis, did not just arise out of a vague scary foreign religion. "It was the US, Europe, and their regional allies in Turkey, Saudi Arabia, Qatar, Kuwait, and United Arab Emirates that created the conditions for the rise of ISIS. They kept the war going in Syria, though it was obvious from 2012 that Assad would not fall."[98] Unfortunately, all these countries are US and Western allies, ultimately supporting the Islamic State—the regime most fearfully associated with a total loss of individual freedom in the world scene.

In the face of this grotesque record, the right wing has its own very traditional picture of the West's history in the world, one which tends not to dwell on the long and undisputed history of taking over countries against their will and using heinous levels of violence to control them. Consider a sparkling article published in *The Wall Street Journal* by foreign affairs professor Walter Mead of Bard College and the libertarian Hudson Institute:

> At bottom, we are witnessing the consequences of a civilization's failure either to overcome or to accommodate the forces of modernity... the Middle East has failed to build economies that allow ordinary people to live with dignity, has failed to build modern political institutions... the Arab world has tried a succession of ideologies and forms of government, and none of them has worked.[99]

What about the legacy of colonial control and looting, and then neocolonialism and support for dictators? Mead has perspective since after all, it's been "One hundred years after the fall of the Ottoman Empire and 50 years since the French left Algeria," while "Britain's defeat of the Ottoman Empire liberated the Arabs from hundreds of years of Turkish rule." To call this a sanitized history hardly describes it — it is a grotesque lie and a hideous farce, but Mead is hardly unusual among conservative intellectuals. Coincidentally, the atrocities that get forgotten and the tyrants who get left out are the ones that would embarrass our home country. Man, what are the odds?

This section has focused on the Middle East, but the role of the imperial powers in shaping most of the modern world in a ruthlessly violent and selfish way goes well beyond that. And since World War II and the US era of global dominance, the US has taken up the imperial role and cast as a threat to freedom every Third World regime that doesn't put private property rights and US military bases first. William Blum's impeccable research on the rich documentary record shows that the US has become a global force that prevents any desperately needed social reform, as he documents in his book *Killing Hope*. Consider a few examples from the American golden age.

In the Congo in Central Africa, the independent post-colonial government led by Patrice Lumumba was undermined by the brutal former colonial power, Belgium, using its still-strong influence and a direct military action to trigger a secession by Katanga, the most economically valuable province and the location of extensive Belgian mineral investments. The US supported this while buying Congolese legislators until the cruel military leader Mobutu took over with Western support. Years later, the congressional Church committee confirmed that Dulles had ordered Lumumba's assassination as "an urgent and prime objective."[100]

Across the Atlantic, Brazil's government was considered to be again too independent and too neutral in the Cold War for Defense Secretary McNamara, and had Communist Party members in some cabinet positions under the elected government of President Joao Goulart. More crucially than typical postcolonial independence, "The Goulart administration, moreover, passed a law limiting the amount of profits multinationals could transmit out of the country, and a subsidiary of ITT was nationalized. Compensation for the takeover was slow in coming..."[101] The Kennedy administration directed development organizations to funnel money into more conservative and pro-US political candidates, cut off previously flowing foreign aid, and a former CIA officer claims an expensive covert propaganda campaign against the regime. The US immediately supported the military coup that followed, in which "Congress was shut down, political opposition was reduced to virtual extinction, habeas corpus for 'political crimes' was suspended, criticism of the president was forbidden by law, labor unions were taken over by government interveners, mounting protests were met by police and military firing into crowds," as Blum documents.[102]

This history is extensive, and readers interested in learning more of this absorbing global history should consult the sources cited here and in the notes. But a short survey should suffice to show that the core capitalist countries of Europe and the US have been archenemies of democracy, and of freedom, except for the hegemonic freedom of elite large-scale property owners. Friedman's thesis, that political freedom will be advanced by his conceived freedom of the marketplace, deserves a lot less respect and remembrance than the army of the dead left behind by the greed of the powers of the world. An army extending, in the eye of the student of history, to the horizon in all directions.

Global Elites and the Man in the Street

The average person globally is now unlikely to feel that they share control of what happens in the world with their fellow men and women, as the Brexit and Trump rebellions illustrate. The popular feeling and reality is that they are subject to powerful elements above them — people, families and organizations that wield enormous power and influence, who trample the freedoms of the common man and woman in the course of their global chess game.

The disagreement is about the nature of these elites. Reading conservative literature, or listening to today's highly influential conservative talk radio and Fox News on US cable, or the Web presence of the far-right European political parties, the listener gets a vague picture of elites. You'll hear about snotty coastal big-city elites, government bureaucratic elites who regulate industry and use "politically correct" speech codes to limit the freedom to use racial language, and, above all, media elites on the network news shows who are biased against the conservative message. These social elements are all relevant and have different forms of power, but what kinds of power they have, how they interact with others and what patterns are dominant never gets explored.

Sometimes, the elitism arising from wealth and market power does come up in the right-wing conversation, but only briefly and through a sharp partisan lens. And as soon as the subject arises, the analysis collapses into confusion. For example, Rush Limbaugh approvingly read a Pat Buchanan article on his radio program, an article in which Buchanan contrasted the evangelical Christian and blue-collar Republican rank-and-file with the "chamber-of-commerce and country-club Republicans," who are more invested in economic issues and tax cuts than the base, and who make up a "Republican Party elite."[103] This kind of analysis is common outside conservative circles, but Limbaugh only brings it up to argue that the party elites should stop criticizing Donald Trump. Afterward, "elites" go back to being found mostly in phrases like "beltway elites" to describe politicians, not "chamber of commerce" elites.

Likewise, the political money pioneer Senator Ted Cruz is willing to allow the existence of a super-wealthy elite 1 percent, using the lingo of the anticapitalist Occupy Wall Street movement. But it can only arise as an adjunct of big government: "The top 1% under President Obama, the millionaires and billionaires that he constantly demagogued, earned a higher share for our income than any year since 1928. Those with power and influence who walk the corridors of power of the Obama administration have gotten fat and happy under big government."[104] And yet the conservative *Wall Street Journal* cites a report by the conservative Koch brothers-founded Tax Foundation, which estimated that Cruz's drastic tax program "delivers its biggest benefits to the top 1% of U.S. households, adding about one-third to their after-tax income."[105] Not surprising, considering the hedge fund billionaires directly running his Super PACs.

The evidence reviewed in this chapter supports the claim made in Chapter 1: there is a spectrum of forms and levels of power, in people and institutions, and the most flexible and unlimited in its potential scale is the power of money and capital. Locally prominent people, politicians and businesses have some power but can be overruled by city or state governments, or a warlord with an army, or a national government, or a large corporation with the threat of capital mobility. Or these all may be misled into disaster by the power of propaganda by a state, corporation or person with the resources to flood the world with its message. These are all forms of power and influence, which we understand to limit human freedom, and holding different amounts of this power makes a person part of an elite among other powerful and influential people, usually with a life of privilege. The fact that the endless day-to-day stream of talk radio and conservative media focuses so obsessively on elites, but only those in government, or among journalists who vote Democrat, or the top labor union leaders, leads us to a similar verdict for Hannity, Levin and Limbaugh as for Friedman and

Hayek: opportunists, working for the interests of power and therefore against the cause of human liberty and freedom.

From this background, we can also evaluate the "libertarianism" represented by this tradition. It's valuable to have a political grouping opposed to any of the large, powerful institutions of our time, as they all require scrutiny and efforts to limit their power. The state, the churches, civil groups, all have some influence and therefore warrant some regular critical attention. But libertarians, as this book shows, have a conspicuous tendency to be critical of *one* of the great power centers of our society, but actively and aggressively insist that *private* power centers are no threat, whether the megabanks or giant corporations or rich families. The result is a skepticism of power that rings very hollow, because it's so selective and in the clear economic interests of its supporters.

This broader view of power and its different dimensions gives us some guidance on global policy issues. Citizens in the US and Europe often react favorably to devolution—proposals to take power from federal government in the US or the European Union system and invest it instead in state governments, or the EU member state parliaments. The appeal, of course, is that of moving decision-making power closer to the people and correspondingly reducing the power of the larger, federal government entity. But the crucial issue is that again, only power in the public sphere is being recognized, and the pivotal leverage of big, international companies never comes up. While a national government can take on a giant corporation on more or less even terms, even a medium-sized company can push state or national governments around by playing one off against the other, thanks to the capital mobility Chapter 1 describes.

People who are frustrated and angry at elites should take a long moment to contemplate where power comes from, its diverse nature, and what kind of policies and social movements for change will leave their kids freer. The best present you can give a kid is freedom and the responsibility to use it well, hopefully including freedom from the codependent relationships among today's elite power centers. Rich elites that would make each of us a chess piece in their power-mongering contest for worldwide market and military dominance.

Endnotes

1. Lawrence Summers, "The Great Liberator,"*The New York Times*, 19 November 2006.
2. Martin Luther King, "Beyond Vietnam," *The Liberatory Thought of Martin Luther King Jr.*, Lanham, MD: Lexington Books, 2012, p.222.
3. Milton and Rose Friedman, *Free to Choose*, New York: Harcourt, 1990, p. 65.
4. *Ibid*, p. 30.
5. Murray Rothbard, *Man, Economy and State with Power and Market*, Auburn, AL: Ludwig von Mises Institute, 2009, p. 984.
6. Miguel Bustillo and Nathan Koppel, "In Texas, Toll Roads Proliferate—and a Backlash Builds,"*The Wall Street Journal*, 20 October 2014.
7. David Harrison, "Donald Trump's Infrastructure Plan Faces Speed Bumps,"*The Wall Street Journal*, 11 November 2016.
8. Miltion Friedman, "Will Freedom Prevail?" *Newsweek*, 19 November 1979.
9. Friedrich Hayek, *The Road to Serfdom*, Chicago: University of Chicago Press, 2007, p. 87.
10. *Ibid*, p. 87-88.
11. Milton and Rose Friedman, *Free to Choose*, New York: Harcourt, 1990, p. 65–6.
12. *Ibid*, p. 140.
13. *Ibid*, p. 36.

14. Charles Beard, *An Economic Interpretation of the Constitution of the United States*, New York: Dover, 2004, p. 14–5.
15. *Ibid*, p. 149.
16. *Ibid*, p. 157–8.
17. Carl Beck, "John Jay and Peter van Schaack," *The Quarterly Journal of the New York State Historical Association*, Vol. 1, No. 1, October 1919, p. 2.
18. Thomas Ferguson, *Golden Rule*, University of Chicago Press, 1995, p. 8.
19. *Ibid*, p. 27.
20. *Ibid*, p. 29, 48.
21. *Ibid*, p. 76.
22. The Center for Responsive Politics [CRP], http://www.opensecrets.org/pres12.
23. *Ibid*, http://www.opensecrets.org/overview.
24. Nicholas Confressore, "Big G.O.P. Donors Stir Senate Runs," *The New York Times*, 11 April 2014.
25. Greg Stohr, "Bloomberg Poll: Americans Want Supreme Court to Turn Off Political Spending Spigot," *Bloomberg*, 28 September 2015.
26. Rebecca Ballhaus, "Super PAC Donors Are Taking Charge,"*The Wall Street Journal*, 31 December 2015. The final paragraph and Conway quote were not included in the print version.
27. CRP, http://www.opensecrets.org/lobby/top.php?indexType=s&showYear=2015.
28. CRP, http://www.opensecrets.org/lobby/top.php?indexType=c&showYear=2015.
29. Roger Martin, "In America, Labor Is Friendless,"*The Harvard Business Review*, 28 August 2014.
30. Martin Gilens and Benjamin Page, "Testing Theories of American Politics: Elites, Interest Groups, and Average Citizens," *Perspectives on Politics*, Vol. 12, No.3, September 2014.

31. Laurie Burkitt, "Rolling Out the Red Carpet," *The Wall Street Journal*, 24 October 2013.

32. Michael Forsythe, "Billionaire Lawmakers Ensure the Rich Are Represented in China's Legislature," *The New York Times*, 2 March 2015.

33. Michael Forsythe and Alan Wong, "Thousands in Hong Kong Rally in Support of China," *The New York Times*, 17 August 2014.

34. David Luhnow, "The Secrets of the World's Richest Man," *The Wall Street Journal*, 4 August 2007.

35. Eduardo Porter, "Mexico's Plutocracy Thrives on Robber-Baron Concessions," *The New York Times*, 27 August 2007.

36. Azam Ahmed, Randal Archibold and Elisabeth Malkin, "Mexico's Richest Man Confronts a New Foe: The State That Helped Make Him Rich," *The New York Times*, 9 August 2016.

37. Ferguson, *Golden Rule*, p. 116.

38. *Ibid*, p. 133–4.

39. Kim Phillips-Fein, *Invisible Hands*, New York: Norton, 2009, p. 95.

40. *Ibid*, p. 31–2, 105.

41. *Ibid*, p. 15; Michael Bordo in Bordo *et al*, *The Defining Moment: The Great Depression and the American Economy in the Twentieth Century*, University of Chicago Press, 1998, p. 292.

42. Phillips-Fein, *Invisible Hands*, p. 41–4, 136.

43. Elton Rayack, *Not So Free to Choose*, New York: Praeger, 1987, p. 119–20.

44. Phillips-Fein, *Invisible Hands*, p. 52.

45. *Ibid*, p. 44, 174, 86.

46. Lewis Powell, "Attack on American Free Enterprise System," US Chamber of Commerce Education Committee, 23 August 1971. Note that the released version, prepared by the Chamber after the confidential original was leaked,

repeats the title as "Attack of American Free Enterprise System," a perhaps more accurate representation of the plan.

47. Robert Brenner, *The Economics of Global Turbulence*, London: Verso, 2006, p. 106, 141; "America's Growing Antibusiness Mood," *Businessweek*, 17 June 1972.

48. Frank Allen, "Carter Rating from Business Drops Further," *The Wall Street Journal*, 30 October 1980.

49. Phillips-Fein, *Invisible Hands*, p. 259–61.

50. Kim Severson and Winnie Hu, "Cut in Food Stamps Forces Hard Choices on Poor," *The New York Times*, 7 November 2013.

51. David Stuckler and Sanjay Basu, *The Body Economic*, New York: Basic Books, 2013, p. 62.

52. *Ibid*, p. 63, 66.

53. *Ibid*, p. 71–72.

54. *Ibid*, p. 84.

55. *Ibid*, p. 90–91.

56. *Ibid*, p. 88, 92.

57. Sheri Fink, "Cuts at W.H.O. Hurt Response to Ebola Crisis," *The New York Times*, 3 September 2014.

58. "What to Cut when Majorities of Americans Support Most Major Government Services?" Harris Interactive, 4 March 2014.

59. Josh Zumbrun, "Boehner Departure Complicates Business Priorities," *The Wall Street Journal*, 25 September 2015.

60. Jia Lynn Yang and Tom Hamburger, "Business groups stand by Boehner, plot against tea party," *The Washington Post*, 17 October 2013.

61. Janet Hook and Patrick O'Connor, "Grass-Roots Anger Transforms Republican Party in Congress and Presidential Campaign," *The Wall Street Journal*, 9 October 2015.

62. Josh Zumbrun, "Boehner Departure Complicates Business Priorities," *The Wall Street Journal*, 25 September 2015.

63. David Krikpatrick, "In a Message to Democrats, Wall St. Sends Cash to G.O.P." *The New York Times*, 7 February 2010.

64. Campbell Robertson and Eric Lipton, "In Alabama Race, a Test of Business Efforts to Derail Tea Party," *The New York Times*, 31 October, 2013.

65. Johnathan Martin, Jim Rutenberg and Jeremy Peters, "Fiscal Crisis Sounds the Charge in G.O.P.'s 'Civil War,'" *The New York Times*, 19 October 2013.

66. *Ibid.*

67. Greg Giroux, "U.S. Chamber Seeks to Oust Boehner Tea Party Antagonists," *Bloomberg*, 28 July 2014.

68. Neil King Jr., "GOP, Business Recast Message," *The Wall Street Journal*, 25 December 2013.

69. Jennifer Drogus, "Timmons: Speaker Boehner Friend of Manufacturing, Tireless Champion of the American Dream," National Association of Manufacturers, 25 September 2015.

70. Kristina Peterson and Siobhan Hughes, "Before Speaker Vote, House Conservatives Drawing Up Wish List," *The Wall Street Journal*, 7 October 2015.

71. Nicole Hong, "U.S. Debt Rating Put on Watch by Fitch," *The Wall Street Journal*, 15 October 2013.

72. Jonathan Weisman and Michael Shear, "The Post-Boehner Congress and Washington's Sense of Dread," *The New York Times*, 26 September 2015; John Carney, "Why Boehner's Resignation Is Good for Markets and the Fed," *The Wall Street Journal*, 25 September 2015.

73. "Letter Regarding Chairman Paul Ryan's FY 2015 Budget," U.S. Chamber of Commerce, 8 April 2014; Jonathan Weisman, "House Republicans Propose Budget With Deep Cuts," *The New York Times*, 17 March 2015.

74. David Herszenhorn and Emmarie Huetteman, "Paul Ryan Wins Backing of Majority in Freedom Caucus for House Speaker," *The New York Times*, 21 October 2015.

75. Rebecca Ballhaus and Brody Mullins, "U.S. Firms Betting

Republicans Maintain Senate Control," *Wall Street Journal*, 6 November 2016.

76. CRP, https://www.opensecrets.org/orgs/recips.php?id=D00 0019798.

77. Sascha Becker, Thiemo Fetzer and Dennis Novy, "Who Voted for Brexit? A Comprehensive District-Level Analysis," University of Warwick Working Paper Series, No. 305, October 2016.

78. Ajay Singh Chaudhary, "What a proper response to Trump's fascism demands: a true ideological left," Quartz, 17 November 2016.

79. Mike Davis, "Not a Revolution—Yet," Verso Blog, 15 November 2016.

80. Bill Fletcher, "Quick reflections on the November 2016 elections," billfletcherjr.com, 9 November 2016.

81. Rebecca Ballhaus and Brody Mullins, "Spending on U.S. Elections Slides for First Time in Recent Political History," *The Wall Street Journal*, 26 October 2016.

82. CRP, https://www.opensecrets.org/pres16/candidate?id=N 00000019 and https://www.opensecrets.org/pres16/candi date.php?id=N00023864, respectively.

83. CRP, https://www.opensecrets.org/pres16/expenditures?id =N00000019.

84. CRP, https://www.opensecrets.org/pres16/expenditures?id =N00023864.

85. Nicholas Confessore and Karen Yourish, "$2 Billion Worth of Free Media Time for Donald Trump," The Upshot, *New York Times*, 15 March 2016.

86. Noam Chomsky, *Year 501*, Boston: South End Press, 1993, p.3.

87. *Ibid*, p. 155–6.

88. *Ibid*, p. 157, 159.

89. Robert Fisk, *The Great War for Civilization*, New York: Vintage, 2007, p. 144–146.

90. *Ibid*, p. 146, 148.
91. *Ibid*, p. 690–1.
92. *Ibid*, p. 207.
93. *Ibid*, p. 62.
94. Patrick Cockburn, *The Rise of the Islamic State*, London: Verso, 2015, p. 4–5.
95. *Ibid*, p. 5–6.
96. Karen Armstrong, "The spread of Wahhabism, and the West's responsibility to the world," *New Statesman*, 26 November 2015.
97. Charles Glass, *Syria Burning*, London: O/R Books, 2015, p. 134.
98. Patrick Cockburn, *The Rise of the Islamic State*, p. 9.
99. Walter Russell Mead, "A Crisis of Two Civilizations," *The Wall Street Journal*, 12–13 September 2015.
100. William Blum, *Killing Hope*, Monroe, ME: Common Courage, 2004, p. 156–158.
101. *Ibid*, p. 163–4.
102. *Ibid*, p. 170.
103. Rush Limbaugh, "What Would Mr. Buckley Think of Mr. Trump?" 14 August, 2015; Patrick Buchanan, "GOP Elites Call For Purge of Trump," RealClearPolitics, 14 August 2015.
104. Ted Cruz, "Ted Cruz in ABC This Week interviews during 2015," 8 February 2015, http://www.ontheissues.org/Archive/2015_ABC_Ted_Cruz.htm.
105. Richard Rubin, "Ted Cruz Tax Plan Would Yield Big Gains to Top 1%—Report," *The Wall Street Journal*, 29 October 2015.

Chapter 4

Heirloom Doom
Freedom of Future Generations

Global warming is socialism by the back door.
George Will[1]

It is difficult to get a man to understand something, when his salary depends upon his not understanding it!
Upton Sinclair[2]

So far, this book has reviewed the dramatic scope of power within market economies — power over the workforce, power over the flow of information, and power over government processes. But one further arena of power and control has to be brought up: power over future generations. If the present generation of men and women have the ability to choose between leaving a wealthier, or environmentally richer, or more peaceful world for future generations, they clearly exercise some power over future populations. And the decisions made through human history, and especially the modern period of capitalism, have rarely been ones that prioritized the welfare of people who must live in the world we leave them.

The term "externalities" refers to the side-costs of economic transactions, where parties that aren't involved in certain market decisions still have to deal with their consequences. It could be an individual annoyed by someone's cigarette smoke, or future generations coping with hugely altered natural environments. Today, our externalities are leaving an awful legacy — multitudes of extinct species, a warming climate, and hugely prevalent pollution from chemicals and plastics. The forms that modern externalities take on need to be reviewed, and the likely consequences for future generations evaluated, before we can fully understand the dynamics of power within capitalism. So let's begin by considering the conservative and libertarian views of the subject and then review the scientific record's projections of the economy of the future.

There Goes the Neighborhood

As usual we begin with the more conservative view, as expressed by its most prominent thinkers. In Milton Friedman's *Capitalism and Freedom*, the problem is described:

> Strictly voluntary exchange is impossible... when actions of individuals have effects on other individuals for which it is not feasible to charge or recompense them. This is the problem of 'neighborhood effects.' An obvious example is the pollution of a stream. The man who pollutes a stream is in effect forcing others to exchange good water for bad... it is not feasible for them, acting individually, to avoid the exchange or to enforce appropriate compensation.[3]

Considering the scale that these "neighborhood effects" or "externalities" are taking on, from traffic smog to species extinction to climate change, some would say that "neighborhood effect" somewhat trivializes the issue. But at least these figures do concede a problem exists, unlike more lightweight intellectuals and shallow right-wing radio show hosts.

Friedrich Hayek even allowed that externalities could warp his cherished symbol of market efficiency, the price system, which transmits information through markets (see Chapter 2). "The price system becomes similarly ineffective when the damage caused to others by certain uses of property cannot be effectively charged to the owner of that property," since:

... there is a divergence between the items which enter into private calculation and those which affect social welfare... Nor can certain harmful effects of deforestation, or some methods of farming, or of the smoke and noise of factories be confined to the owner of the property in question or to those who are willing to submit to the damage for an agreed compensation.[4]

After the denial of capitalism's problems from these thinkers in this book's previous chapters, these are pretty candid concessions! Just recognizing the issue isstrong meat from the two most prominent conservative economists of the twentieth century.

However, the tendency in this school is often to acknowledge the undeniable existence of these economic side-effects, but then to move on quickly to minimizing them and disparaging any government attempts to actually limit or fix them. In *Free to Choose*, Milton and Rose Friedman wrote that indeed, "Almost everything we do has some third-party effects, however small and however remote," and they correctly recognize an important aspect of externalities: "The primary source of significant third-party effects of private actions is the difficulty of identifying the external costs or benefits."[5] It's very difficult to say for sure exactly how much your cigarette smoking has affected the health of your family, for example, and whether Junior's asthma is largely because of your two-packs-a-day or because of air pollution from the nearby highway. So far, fair enough.

But the Friedmans veer away sharply with their following demand that for anyone supporting legal limits to things like public smoking or lead-emitting car exhaust, "the burden of proof should be on its proponents."[6] After conceding the reality and prevalence of externalities, and specifically agreeing that they are frequently challenging to quantify in terms of their effects, or to definitively prove them harmful to particular individuals, we're told we should still generally oppose any public policy. The reality of the issue is briefly accepted, but the resulting popular desire for political action is immediately denied.

On the other hand, people who take externalities seriously, including many scientists and public health specialists, are more likely to support a "precautionary principle," suggesting a default posture of caution before producing or consuming a new commodity on a very large scale. But this would happen to be an obstacle to commerce in new commodities and so libertarian intellectuals reliably oppose it; apparently yet another instance of right-wing intellectuals showing opportunistic tendencies.

The Friedmans double down, claiming that "The environmental movement is responsible for one of the most rapidly growing areas of federal intervention. The Environmental Protection Agency... has been granted increasing power and authority." The scope of the issue has no specifics in their description, and notably in a book that often argues for balancing costs and benefits, no benefits of EPA policies are brought up, only discussions of costly budgets and staff figures. And interestingly for writers who completely, totally neglect to cite any scientists or experts on public health, they claim "Public discussion of the environmental issue is frequently characterized more by emotion than reason."[7] An emotion-driven debate to which they are willing to contribute, apparently.

Their conclusion therefore ignores the overwhelming flow of scientific research on environmental side-effects of industrial capitalism (reviewed below), and take their political shot for Reaganite libertarian anti-regulation.

This is a very brief treatment of an extremely important and far-reaching problem... Perhaps it may also lead to a second look at the performance of market mechanisms in areas where they admittedly operate imperfectly. The imperfect market may, after all, do as well or better than the imperfect government. In pollution, such a look would bring many surprises.[8]

Maybe one of these "surprises" will be that scientists are fretfully anticipating a series of "global-scale failures" owing to the enormous scale of today's externalities.[9] It's beyond "imperfect" and well beyond a neighborhood's reach.

Other conservatives are more cautious about extracting capital from natural resources, but no less committed to it. Oxford economist Paul Collier wrote in his book *The Plundered Planet* that yes, natural resources are precious and potentially fragile, but that our obligation is only to be custodians of natural assets, meaning "We are ethically obliged to pass on to future generations the equivalent value of the natural assets that we were bequeathed in the past."[10] As long as the value derived from exploiting nature is not immediately consumed (or "plundered"), then we are behaving responsibly.

This means that nature is seen as a capital asset exchangeable for money and indeed Collier comments that "Biodiversity is a good thing, but within the context of our survival, not as an end in itself. We are not here to serve nature; nature is here to serve us." Likewise, he claims "natural substances only acquire value as a result of technological discoveries," and scientists or activists who support the conservation of natural systems "hate industrial capitalism," are somehow both Marxist and monarchist, and "sense the opportunity to refresh the guilt-ridden colonialist hangover."[11] This man is considered a bold thinker in today's neoliberal political setting.

More liberal "green" figures tend to limit themselves to what can be achieved by encouraging businesses to be more interested in sustainability—the ability of an economy to function indefinitely by not overconsuming natural resources or over-polluting. Among the most prominent liberal "green" thinkers is Paul Hawken, who writes early in his influential *The*

Ecology of Commerce that "business is destroying the world, no one does it better," and claims "The market of today is free but in an entirely different way, because its freedom is immune to community accountability. The primary freedom of the modern, global marketplace is that companies can grow unremittingly."[12] Certainly Collier or the other conservatives reviewed here could be accused of seeing freedom in these terms. So Hawken says that while capitalism creates a freedom for large institutions to grow and prosper, this is a disservice to others—the "hegemonic freedom" that really means power over people, as discussed in Chapter 1.

More cuttingly, he reminds us that "to redesign or start up a business that maintains a holistic relationship between economy and ecology handicaps the entrepreneur financially since she bears the costs of the additional responsibilities that she has assumed and her competitors have shunned," a problem of "the current economic system." Indeed, "the sheer size of the largest corporations tends to grant them the political and economic power to externalize costs that should be properly absorbed by the company."[13] Yet, despite all this, Hawken goes on to suggest that sustainability can be achieved by relatively simple government regulations like green taxes, which would tax firms in rough proportion to their pollution.

Hawken further concedes elsewhere in the text that "Concentrated political and economic power is a major deterrent to establishing green taxes and other features of a restorative economy." And more broadly, as we saw in in Chapter 3, any reforms demanded by the public and placed on capital's liberty by elected representatives can be undermined and watered down over time, just as the broad New Deal programs of income supports and industrial regulation were. Hawken also expects firms to voluntarily reconfigure their entire business models to accommodate habitat conservation and pollution limitation, despite the pressure from Wall Street to maintain profitability.

As he perhaps accurately says, "No other institution in the modern world is powerful enough to foster the necessary material and economic changes."[14] Which also implies no other institution is powerful enough to successfully fight *against* the necessary changes. For as we've seen, institutions don't often make voluntary changes adverse to their material well-being.

For their part, left-wing analysts have been willing to call for more fundamental social changes to cope with the towering problems created by our limitless economic growth. Socialist sociologist John Bellamy Foster wrote thoughtfully about these subjects, questioning:

> The dominant conception of human freedom. For centuries our society has seen freedom as a mechanical outgrowth of the technological domination of nature, and of a social arrangement in which each individual is encouraged to pursue his or her own self-interest with no consideration of the larger natural or social repercussions. Environmental protection, it is feared, would set limits both on the freedom of human beings to exploit the earth's resources, and on the freedom of individuals to pursue their own immediate material gain.[15]

He supports "a human relation to nature that is based on 'freedom in general': not the freedom to exclude others from a genuine relation to nature and the full development of life's possibilities; but rather the freedom of all to share in life's development as part of an organic community."[16] So Foster, writing from the Left, considers people to have a positive freedom to take part in enjoying the richness of nature.

In order to resolve which side of this argument is more sensible, we'll have to consider what actual scientists say about these subjects.

Inherit the Whirlwind

It's a striking fact about today's environmental arguments that people often feel quite entitled to insist upon questions of ecological fact, without even the slightest familiarity with the current state of science on the subject. Few people would think they know better than their doctor or an architect, but with scientific subjects that bear on money issues, suddenly everyone is a skeptical thinker and casts themselves as brave rebels against the scientific consensus.

A great way to cut the crap in any argument about climate or ecology is to simply ask your confident debate partner what was the last scientific paper they read about their claim. More often than not, your friend will be relying on a source that does not directly refer to any scientific findings, let alone actual scientific research material itself, before shooting off their mouths. We can avoid this pitfall by sampling the current research.

Doing so becomes alarming quickly. A major debate in the field is the nature of the "Anthropocene," a newly designated geological period, based on the rise of humanity and our unprecedented powers to reshape local environments and global ecological systems. The debate has recently moved past the stage of argument over whether or not this new period exists, since the large majority of Earth scientists now find the giant impact of humanity adequately transformative worldwide, and geologically visible enough, to qualify as its own geological era. The debate now addresses the Anthropocene's nature and the exact timing of it, for example in a 2016 paper for the prestigious US journal *Science* by a large global team of chemists, geologists, archaeologists, oceanographers and biologists.[17] The paper discusses different possible times to designate the start of the period, from the spike in global population in the eighteenth century, or from the rise of polluting emissions during the Industrial Revolution in the nineteenth, or using the appearance in the record of "Novel markers, such as concrete, plastics, global black carbon, and plutonium (Pu) fallout." It suggests that from the perspective of new geological markers, "The start of the Anthropocene may thus be defined... with the detonation of the Trinity atomic device at Alamogordo, New Mexico, on 16 July 1945 CE." Not an auspicious start to the era named for us!

Other scientists disagree within the rules of scientific debate, with some supporting earlier starts and another team suggesting "Only beyond the mid-20th century is there clear evidence for fundamental shifts in the state and functioning of the Earth System that are beyond the range of variability of the Holocene and driven by human activities."[18] The scientific conversation continues, but clearly within a broad agreement that a new era has arrived in which human economics has become a driving force transforming the planetary system. Again, we're redefining geological epochs here—reaching way beyond what can be called "neighborhood effects."

These issues are often discussed around the concept of sustainability—the ability, referred to earlier, of a society to sustain itself indefinitely on available resources, rather than exhausting them or choking on its own accumulated pollution. This subject can be written large or small—smaller-scale examples include the plunging groundwater levels in the US plains states, where ancient freshwater aquifers are falling fast as farmers use them to irrigate their crops. The High Plains Aquifer's southern reaches are "increasingly tapped out, drained by ever more intensive farming and, lately, by drought," *The New York Times* reports. "And when the groundwater runs out, it is gone for good. Refilling the aquifer would require hundreds, if not thousands, of years of rains... Most of the creeks and rivers that once veined the land have dried up as 60 years of pumping have pulled groundwater levels down by scores and even hundreds of feet."[19] This kind of overuse of a readily accessed but limited resource, often called a "common resource," is a frequently seen and widely recognized limit of the market system.

Other relatively small-scale examples of the rising anthropogenic era include great icons of global capitalism — not just the famously prosperous US heartland, but Cerro Rico, one of the symbols of early colonialism, is literally collapsing from the issue. Cerro Rico is a mountain in Bolivia, famous for its incredibly rich silver deposits. These major precious metal deposits had a hugely crucial economic effect under the cruel Spanish Empire, bringing enough coinage into Europe that "It fueled the early growth of European capitalism," as the press reminds us, and indeed the mountain is depicted on Bolivia's national flag.[20] But now the silver deposits have been mined so aggressively and exhaustively that the top of the mountain is in danger of collapse.

The government agency in charge of mining allows private firms to run the mines since silver prices crashed decades ago, so competitive forces have led them to overexploit the deposits, beyond a level that might be sustained even over the medium term. And of course the usual bargaining power advantage of capital owners (reviewed in Chapter 1) applies here, whether the operator is the government, private companies or the Spanish Empire: "For all the wealth the mountain generated, the misery outpaced it a hundredfold. The Spanish used Indians, or slaves brought from Africa, to work in the mines in brutal conditions. The death toll was high," and today engineers report "accidents were frequent and often fatal and that the bodies of dead miners, frequently migrants from the countryside, were often taken straight to their villages for burial so the deaths did not come to the attention of local officials or mining regulators."

But beyond these smaller-scale examples, the issue of sustainability in the Anthropocene has a number of far larger-scale dimensions, two of which we'll look at here — mass extinction and climate change. Mass extinction refers to large waves of species extinctions, in which many separate species of animals, plants or microorganisms have their numbers fall below the level that can maintain them as a population, and the species ceases to exist. Extinction is a normal process occurring in natural habitats at a relatively regular, measured pace, but the geological record is punctuated with "mass extinction events," in which great numbers of species disappear in a short timespan. The most famous of these is the extinction of the dinosaurs and the ecosystems associated with them at the end of the Cretaceous period, likely owing to a major planetary impact by a large meteor or comet. But today, it is broadly agreed by biologists and other scientists that the planet is about to enter, or already has, a sixth global extinction event, only this one is caused by human activity and the global Anthropocene.

As usual, people enjoy spouting opinions about this issue without doing much (or any) research into the current scientific literature on the subject, and laugh off the spreading extinctions of hundreds of species of little-known frogs or obscure sea life. But the scientists take the subject much more seriously and one of their major findings is that today's crash in the global richness of species (or "biodiversity") is the result of destruction of the natural habitat that species live among.

This includes the most charismatic species, like the "megafauna," or large animals like giraffes and bears. A large team of biologists recently wrote in the journal *BioScience* that:

... 59% of the world's largest carnivores... and 60% of the world's largest herbivores... are classified as threatened with extinction on the International Union for the Conservation of Nature (IUCN) Red List... Species at risk of extinction include some of the world's most iconic animals—such as gorillas, rhinos, and big cats—and unfortunately, they are vanishing just as science is discovering their essential ecological roles.[21]

Or consider forests. An outstanding 2015 study of global forest landscapes by a large team of life scientists discovered that forest stands have become so diminished and fragmented by human development that, to their horror,

> Nearly 20% of the world's remaining forest is within 100 m of an edge—in close proximity to agricultural, urban, or other modified environments where impacts on forest ecosystems are most severe. More than 70% of the world's forests are within 1 km of a forest edge. Thus, most forests are well within the range where human activities, altered microclimate, and nonforest species may influence and degrade forest ecosystems... across experiments spanning numerous studies and ecosystems, fragmentation consistently degraded ecosystems, reducing species persistence, species richness, nutrient retention, trophic dynamics, and, in more isolated fragments, movement.[22]

Another impeccably credentialed cadre of scientists note that the same processes of destruction and degradation of habitat have been happening on land environments for far longer than ocean ecosystems, but recent centuries have seen the rise of extremely serious deterioration in the seas also. They note that "Current ocean trends, coupled with terrestrial defaunation [loss of animal species] lessons, suggest that marine defaunation rates will rapidly intensify as human use of the oceans industrializes."[23] The oceans are under a large number of stresses, from rising catches of large fish to growing "dead zones" caused by fertilizer runoff to plastic and chemical pollution to escalating acidity. This "industrialization" of the seas means, among many other things, a plunging availability of habitat for the unbelievable variety of marine life forms.

Elizabeth Kolbert's popular book *The Sixth Extinction* puts a more intimate face on the dry scientific facts of our mass extinction, recording for example the words of an Australian scientist studying the reef systems of the Pacific: "Yet here I am today, humbled to have spent the most productive scientific years of my life around the rich wonders of the underwater world, and utterly convinced that they will not be there for our children's children to enjoy."[24]

Other research in *Science* estimates "land use and related pressures have already reduced local biodiversity intactness — the average proportion of natural biodiversity remaining in local ecosystems — beyond its recently proposed planetary boundary across 58.1% of the world's land surface, where 71.4% of the human population live."[25] The "boundary" refers to estimates of the "safe limit" beyond which biodiversity and species richness may crash and be irretrievable.

But the newest contributor to mass extinction trends is global climate change, which contributes modestly at the moment, but is projected to grow dramatically. A conservative study in *Science* suggests an outcome, if we follow our current trajectory, that on its own "climate change threatens one in six species (16%)."[26] Climate change is the gradual evolution of global temperatures over time, dominated in the last few centuries by the giant growth of greenhouse gases, which trap heat in the Earth's atmosphere, from human industry and agriculture. These gases, including carbon dioxide from smokestacks and car tailpipes and methane from farming, allow the Sun's radiation in but are partially opaque to the infrared radiation that the Earth reflects back into space. This raises overall temperatures, just like in a greenhouse.

The subject of climate change, more than any other subject, is afflicted by people who've heard only a few minutes of one-sided commentary but have decided they know better than the scientists, and will claim there's no scientific "consensus," or broad agreement, about the phenomenon. However, researchers have examined this specific issue and their findings are striking. Scientists studying the subject for *Environmental Research*

Letters found "The consensus that humans are causing recent global warming is shared by 90%–100% of publishing climate scientists" according to a series of reviews of abstracts of climate research papers and separate surveys of authors of these papers themselves.[27] One of the papers included in that analysis examined an amazing 11,944 climate-relevant paper abstracts, showing a high level of professional consensus. "Among abstracts expressing a position on [anthropogenic global warming], 97.1% endorsed the consensus positions that humans are causing global warming... we invited authors to rate their own papers... 97.2% endorsed the consensus... Our analysis indicates that the number of papers rejecting the consensus on AGW is a vanishingly small proportion of the published research."[28]

Indeed, even while the great firms of the energy industry were arguing publicly that climate scientists were mistaken, their own engineers were taking climate change and sea-level rise seriously in their designs. Exxon, Shell, BP and others formed the Global Climate Coalition with a mission of casting doubt on the science of global climate change. The *Los Angeles Times* reports that:

… one company, Exxon, made a strategic decision in the late 1980s to publicly emphasize doubt and uncertainty regarding climate change science even as its internal research embraced the growing scientific consensus... In 1989, before Shell Oil joined the Global Climate Coalition, the company announced it was redesigning a $3-billion North Sea natural gas platform that it had been developing for years. The reason it gave: Sea levels were going to rise as a result of global warming. The original design called for the platform to sit 30 meters above the ocean's surface, but the company decided to raise it by a meter or two.[29]

So the firms went on funding public denial, despite their own better advice. The powerful International Monetary Fund (IMF) takes the issue seriously also. They estimated the yearly "external" costs of using fossil fuels, counting effects on public health and the various environmental ramifications, come to a stupefying $5 trillion per year.[30] This constitutes "one of the biggest externalities ever estimated," *The Wall Street Journal* reports, and again quite beyond Friedman's quaint "neighborhood effects."

But the corporate climate-denying organizations, typical of the associations of powerful firms reviewed in Chapter 1, was fairly effective. A fascinating research article published in the prestigious *Proceedings of the National Academy of the Sciences* applied an analysis algorithm to a giant number of texts discussing climate and concluded "organizations with corporate funding were more likely to have written and disseminated texts meant to polarize the climate change issue." And further, "corporate funding influences the actual thematic content of these polarization efforts," so that rather than a non-partisan scientific subject, the issue is treated like a "polarized" political issue, with corporate-driven talking points always present. The paper empirically addresses "the actual social arrangements within which large-scale scientific (mis)information is generated, and the important role private funding plays in shaping the actual ideological content of scientific information that is written and amplified."[31]

And the commercial media, for their part, have gone on treating the issue as a debatable political subject rather than increasingly settled science. As FAIR and other media monitors have documented, their various current affairs programs and hosts have reliably fought against accepting these well-established scientific conclusions, unlike their usual more accepting pattern of reporting on cutting-edge science news.[32] Through this policy, they have followed their institutional obligation not to offend the large corporations that are their advertisers, as well as the class interests of the wealthy families and stockholders that own all these corporations. Exactly the kind of thing George Orwell suggested would happen, back in Chapter 2.

The combination of corporate funding to deny the issue, and obedient dissembling by the commercial media, has had an effect. Studies, for example by Yale researchers, have found that just 12 percent of Americans believe (correctly) that over 90 percent of relevant scientists have reached the conclusion of human-caused global climate change, while 14 percent think less than half of scientists believe this. Barely more Americans believe climate change is human-caused than a naturally occurring fluctuation.[33]

Meanwhile, not only the energy industry itself, but also the rest of the business world have realized that scientists have settled the basic issue and are taking it seriously. The insurance industry, long looked to as the business segment that would wake the rest of the economy up to the issue since it would have to pay the costs of rising seas and temperatures, has said little on the subject. Business reporting has found that "Most insurers, including the reinsurance companies that bear much of the ultimate risk in the industry, have little time for the arguments heard in some right-wing circles that climate change isn't happening, and are quite comfortable with the scientific consensus." However, insurance data-management firms argue that "insurers haven't changed their tune because... they haven't yet experienced hefty, sustained losses attributable to climate change."[34] So the industry's not fooled by "politicized science," which is nice, but it won't help shift the debate until the huge costs are already here.

As we'll explore next, the very real consequences of the climate change we're now largely committed to, have the real potential to contribute to our many global crises, quite plausibly to the extent of destroying civilization. Now, this book has argued that concentrated power is opposed to human freedom, which everyone basically agrees with, and that capitalist institutions and classes wield a great deal of that power, which few in prominent intellectual positions agree with. But here we're looking at the ability of capitalists who are responsible for our planet-transforming energy emissions to keep the issue from being seen by the public as basic science, even though they knew otherwise.

Exxon-Mobil CEO Rex Tillerson, prior to being elevated to the Trump administration's State Secretary, commented "We have spent our entire existence adapting, OK? So we will adapt to this. Changes to weather patterns that move crops around— we'll adapt to that. It's an engineering problem, and it has engineering solutions."[35] This adaptation is expected to cost trillions and mean the loss of significant ecological functioning, but figures like Tillerson and the giant of capital he ran were able to bring it upon us.

What is the ultimate power? I say to you, it is the power to doom the houses of man.

Serfdom 2100

With this understanding of the power involved in the twenty-first century's environmental issues, we can look at the broader ramifications for freedom itself. The issue of freedom arises from the plain reality that our economic system is not sustainable, meaning that on its current course society will exhaust its precious resources, get cooked by climate change and become poisoned by its own pollution. If this comes to pass, it unavoidably means that future generations will not have access to the basic functioning systems we rely on today, will not have the ability to enjoy adequate fresh air and water, and will not be able to enjoy the benefits of biodiversity or "ecosystem services" like pollution filtering or the simple aesthetic value of nature.

This possible future diminishment or collapse of natural systems means men and women of the future will not have the freedom to benefit from or enjoy such ecological services—a major loss of positive freedom, the liberty to partake in valuable natural systems. When future species are extinct, temperatures dramatically higher, sea levels elevated, pollution-absorbing capacity exhausted and basic natural processes like decomposition or pollination falling apart, humanity will have dramatically limited freedom to enjoy the foundations of life. Indeed, since this process has been going on for many centuries, we ourselves enjoy less positive ecological freedom than our ancestors, who might have been able to contemplate now extinct animals and now vanished landscapes. Our compensation is a richer material economy built from the consumption of these systems; although as we've seen, not everyone gets to share in the spoils. And if the processes of capitalism continue, we're likely to reach tipping points where more material wealth will be totally unable to compensate for huge losses of our natural heritage.

To grasp the grave risks to liberty from our economic trajectory, it's useful to choose a point in the future to evaluate the loss of the freedom to benefit from nature. Many scientific and social studies of environmental deterioration and social adaptation to it use the end of the twenty-first century as a benchmark, and so the year 2100 is convenient as a milepost to gauge the future we're looking at, if the world's scientists are any guide. Think of it as a spoiler alert for the freedom your grandkids will enjoy.

The broadest environmental issue today is global climate change and its most fundamental consequence is the basic rise in average temperatures already recorded by the giant majority of scientists. Exactly how quickly the atmosphere and oceans will warm, and what parts of the planet will warm when, are subject to natural scientific debate. But the benchmark projections of temperature increase come from the IPCC, the Intergovernmental Panel on Climate Change, made up of climate scientists, geologists, meteorologists and oceanographers from around the world. The IPCC generally is actually conservative in its conclusions, in part owing to government influence, which prefers not to release alarming information, but its cautious conclusions can be legitimately described as representing a major benchmark for the scientific consensus on climate change.

The IPCC's most recent report, the *Climate Change 2014 Synthesis Report*, details its expectations for the climate change of the twenty-first century. Their estimates for global mean temperature increase range by 2100 from 1 to 3.7 degrees Celsius (or 1.8 to 6.6 degrees Fahrenheit).[36] These warming projections have extremely serious ramifications, way beyond the uncomfortable heat and occasional flooding people casually imagine.

For terrestrial conditions come 2100, scientists writing in the prominent journal *PLOS Biology* summarize their work in an abstract:

> We show that although the global mean number of days above freezing will increase by up to 7% by 2100 under 'business as usual'... suitable growing days will actually decrease globally by up to 11% when other climatic variables that limit plant growth are considered (i.e., temperature, water availability, and solar radiation)... Notably, tropical areas could lose up to 200 plant growing days per year.[37]

This potentially catastrophic decline in plant growth is expected to arise mainly from hotter peak temperatures and decreased water availability. Beside this global trend, severe regional desiccation (or drying-out) is expected, for example in the US southwest, which is believed to have an over 80 percent chance of an extreme drought during 2050 to 2099, researchers have written in *Science Advances*.[38] Separate research indicates by mid-century, tens of millions of Americans will endure "smoke waves" caused by the huge plumes of fine smoke and ash billowing out from the giant western wild fires promoted by the projected dryness and summer heat.[39]

Beyond the obviously crucial issue of food production and drought, in regions that are hot to begin with, the coming century looks to be especially unkind. A paper in *Nature Climate Change* observes that while the human body can adapt to high temperature conditions through increased respiration and sweating, there are natural limits to this process, and by 2100 extremities of "temperature in the region around the Arabian Gulf are likely to approach and exceed this critical threshold under the business-as-usual scenario of future greenhouse gas concentrations."[40] This means that during the summer it will be impossible to live outdoors in much of the Middle East, a development "likely to severely impact human habitability in the future." In other words, Europe hasn't even seen its real refugee crisis yet.

These projections are built upon the IPCC's "business as usual" scenario, a plausible choice given the world's foot-dragging on even today's wimpy emissions treaties. The effects are likely to take us by surprise, despite all the warnings of scientists, as researchers in *Science* note this century's climate warming "is comparable in magnitude to that of the largest global changes in the past 65 million years but is orders of magnitude more rapid."[41] They conclude that "The combination of high climate-change velocity and multi-dimensional human fragmentation will present terrestrial ecosystems with an environment that is unprecedented in recent evolutionary history." Other research in *PNAS* predicts "future climate states with no current analog and the disappearance of some extant climates... Novel climates are projected to develop primarily in the tropics and subtropics, whereas disappearing climates are concentrated in tropical montane regions and the poleward portions of continents."[42] They suggest up to nearly half "of the Earth's terrestrial surface may respectively experience novel and disappearing climates by 2100 AD."

That combination of habitat fragmentation, and the decline of other natural systems owing to climate disruption, means that when *Science* ran a research article by a very large team of scientists that developed "Global Biodiversity Scenarios for the Year 2100," they found that climate was the second most important driver of "biodiversity change," after human land-use change.[43] They found "There is clear evidence for nonlinearities and synergistic interactions among many of the global change drivers." Surprising combinations of effects like these mean that scenarios and projections for the future are not real predictions, because of the complicated nature of the systems being studied. These earnest technical papers are projections based on present observation and current best scientific understanding, not guaranteed for sure, but the best we have.

Less complicated than precisely which of our "externalities" is most responsible for mass extinction is the relatively simple subject of sea-level rise. The IPCC has corresponding estimates of expected sea-level rise to go with its temperature-increase projections, ranging from 0.4 to 0.63 meters (1.3 to 2.0 feet).[44] The median and upper projections would mean serious disruption to all coastal and low-lying areas, which of course are where human civilization has developed most of its largest cities and biggest investments.

Other scientists base their projections on higher sea levels, in part because more recent work suggests that the worldwide "climate sensitivity," or the amount of climate-system warming for a given amount of carbon emissions, is recently appearing to be toward the higher end of the IPCC's projections. Work published in the *Journal of Climate* indicates this is largely owing to the tendency of tropical clouds to thin out more as warming continues, thus adding to the warming per ton of CO_2.[45] Research in the journal *Nature*, using such higher sea-level increases, projects that:

... a 2100 SLR [Sea Level Rise] of 0.9m places a land area projected to house 4.2 million people at risk of inundation, whereas 1.8m affects 13.1 million people—approximately two times larger than indicated by current populations. These results suggest that the absence of protective measures could lead to US population movements of a magnitude similar to the twentieth century Great Migration of African-Americans.[46]

Pretty high stakes, but as we saw above the power of the energy industry has been enough to force this reality on us.

Exactly how this will play out for any specific coastal region is unclear, owing to the large number of local variables, but some estimates have been made. Adding to the pressures on a crucial Arab country, "Without adaptation, a rise by 0.5m would displace 3.8 million people in the most fertile part of the Nile River Delta," reports an article in *Science*; others observe a giant increase in the likelihood and scale of future floods on the US East Coast.[47] Beside the direct loss of real property values, economists project financial asset losses from twenty-first century climate change in the trillions of dollars.

Below the rising sea surface, losses from this out-of-control climate extend to ocean-based commerce and food production. A large team of scientists in *PLOS Biology* expected a drop in phytoplankton concentrations, which is menacing if you consider that the tiny microorganisms jointly called plankton are a base of the entire marine food chain. "By 2100, projected changes in temperature, dissolved oxygen, pH, and primary food supply vary significantly among regions," but the researchers report "robust" confidence in the upward trend of ocean temperature, and the downward trend of oxygen and pH.[48]

Indeed, the oceans appear to be in for a terrible beating over this century. Scientists in *Nature* expect a wide occurrence of elevated CO_2 levels or "hypercapnia," which can produce behavioral and neurological changes in sea animals. "We predict that the present-day amplitude of the natural oscillations in oceanic CO_2 concentration will be amplified by up to tenfold in some regions by 2100." This means "major fisheries" may be exposed and horrifyingly, "hypercapnia is expected in up to half the surface ocean by 2100, assuming a high-emissions scenario."[49] Indeed, between ocean warming, acidification, hypercapnia and other stressors, biologists writing in *Science* assembled a model projecting "the global collapse of all taxa currently fished by the mid-21st century," and found "rates of resource collapse increased and recovery potential, stability, and water quality decreased exponentially with declining diversity."[50]

Kolbert's book describes the decline of sea organisms that rely on calcium shells or plates, including starfish, clams, barnacles and coral. These organisms are vulnerable to the "acidification" of the world's oceans, since the carbon dioxide emitted as an externality by our capitalist economy chemically dissociates in seawater into acidic compounds. This acid has built up in the seas as our exponential Industrial Revolution has continued, to the point where the legendary Great Barrier Reef of Australia is projected to be a dead rubble pile by 2050. As the problem has continued, marine biologists have identified a threshold level of pH=7.8, at which "the ecosystem starts to crash… which is what we're expecting to happen by 2100."[51]

Of course this is just for the coming century and the really long-term effects are far worse. For example, a report in *PNAS* indicates that while projections of sea-level rise through 2100 are generally a meter or less, the climate system's long-term adjustments are "roughly an order to magnitude higher."[52] This means that "unabated carbon emissions up to the year 2100 would commit an eventual global sea-level rise of 4.2-9.9 m… we find that land that is home to more than 20 million people is implicated and is widely distributed among different states and coasts." So the full impacts of climate change have a far longer horizon than the twenty-first century. Among those potential coastal losses are several World Heritage sites—the locations of special global historical or cultural significance designated by UNESCO, the United Nations cultural body. In this longer run of millennial time, scientists expect 136 of these precious structures or locations will be impacted, including some of humanity's most beautiful and important monuments, buildings, neighborhoods and ruins that would be sinking or submerged.[53]

All these issues are intimately connected to issues of freedom. At the least, there is an issue of positive freedom, the "freedom to" do different things, in the sense that the irrevocable changes to the world made in our time will strip future generations of the freedom to enjoy nature. Many men and women of the future may not be free to drink clean water, or to explore rich, thriving coral reefs, or catch the fish that mature among them. They will be unable to enjoy the simple splendor of natural settings and processes that we presently take for granted, even in their diminished state.

Indeed, are we not currently limited in our freedom owing to the decisions of our ancestors? We're not free to observe a pod of the near extinct Right Whale or the totally extinct Giant Sloth. Right now, millions globally lack drinkable water or have their homes lost to growing deserts, all the result of economic decisions made by past generations. These are irrevocable changes and more than losing pretty megafauna, it's the loss of the basic systems that include them, and on which we rely, that's important here. Seen through the lens of the long-term effects of our decisions, our descendants look less likely to have built heaven on Earth and more like the unfree serfs of the Middle Ages, their standards of living dramatically cut down and their freedoms sharply pulled back, but now thanks to decisions made by their forebears in our times.

At other times, the relationship of ecology and freedom is more synchronized. In 2014, 7500 gallons of a synthetic chemical used in coal processing leaked from a storage tank into the Elk River in West Virginia, making the water reek of licorice and forcing 300,000 people to avoid the poisoned water for drinking or cleaning. *The New York Times* observed that efforts to encourage the state to adopt strong environmental regulations "died a quiet death with barely any consideration by state and local lawmakers," while *The Wall Street Journal* found the "Chemical-Spill Site Avoided Broad Regulatory Scrutiny," typical in the neoliberal Age of Friedman.[54] They observed that "The chemical that leaked into the river, 4-methylcyclohexane methanol, isn't closely tracked by federal programs. Before last week's spill, a state regulator said environmental inspectors hadn't visited the site since 1991." The chemical company whose tank ruptured? Freedom Industries Inc.

When future generations look at the world we've left them, will they think back on our era as representing the freest time for people? Or will they see our short-term-based actions, creating huge ecological "debts" for them to pay, as closer to how the great US intellectual and freed slave Frederick Douglass saw the "boasted liberty" of slave owners in the old South: "an unholy license."[55] That sounds to me how future generations will see some of our liberties, if we proceed along our present course.

So for our next and final chapter, let's pivot to the positive and take up the question of how we can avoid plunging into the abyss that the world's scientists are telling us is dead ahead.

Endnotes

1. Jamie Weinstein, "George Will Calls Global Warming 'A Religion,' 'Socialism By the Back Door,'" *The Daily Caller*, 27 April 2014.
2. Upton Sinclair, *I Candidate for Governor: And How I Got Licked*, Berkeley and Los Angeles, CA: University of California Press, 1934, p.109.

3. Milton Friedman, *Capitalism and Freedom*, Chicago, IL: University of Chicago Press, 2002, p. 30.
4. Friedrich Hayek, *The Road to Serfdom*, Chicago: University of Chicago Press, 2007, p. 87.
5. Milton and Rose Friedman, *Free to Choose*, New York: Harcourt, 1990, p. 31.
6. *Ibid*, p. 32.
7. *Ibid*, p. 213, 214.
8. *Ibid*, p. 218.
9. Brian Walker *et al*, "Looming Global-Scale Failures and Missing Institutions," *Science*, Vol. 325, No. 5946, 11 September 2009.
10. Paul Collier, *The Plundered Planet*, New York: Oxford University Press, 2010, p. 11.
11. *Ibid*, p. 32, 18, 195.
12. Paul Hawken, *The Ecology of Commerce*, New York: Harper, 2010, p. xvii, 88.
13. *Ibid*, p. 42, 108.
14. *Ibid*, p. 103, 20.
15. John Bellamy Foster, *Ecology Against Capitalism*, New York: Monthly Review Press, 2002, p. 52.
16. *Ibid*, p. 58–9.
17. Colin Waters *et al*, "The Anthropocene is functionally and stratigraphically distinct from the Holocene," *Science*, Vol. 351, No. 6269, 8 January 2016.
18. Will Steffen *et al*, "The trajectory of the Anthropocene: The Great Acceleration," *The Anthropocene Review*, Vol. 2, No. 1, April 2015.
19. Michael Wines, "Wells Dry, Fertile Plains Turn to Dust," *The New York Times*, 19 May 2013.
20. William Neuman, "For Miners, Increasing Risk on a Mountain at the Heart of Bolivia's Identity," *The New York Times*, 16 September 2014.
21. William Ripple *et al*, "Saving the World's Terrestrial

Megafauna," *BioScience*, 27 July 2016.

22. Nick Haddad, "Habitat fragmentation and its lasting impact on Earth's ecosystems," *Science Advances*, Vol. 1, No. 2, 20 March 2015.

23. Douglas McCauley *et al*, "Marine defaunation: Animal loss in the global ocean," *Science*, Vol. 347, No. 6219, 16 January 2015.

24. Elizabeth Kolbert, *The Sixth Extinction*, New York: Henry Holt, 2014, p. 138.

25. Tim Newbold *et al*, "Has land use pushed terrestrial biodiversity beyond the planetary boundary? A global assessment," *Science*, Vol. 353, No. 6296, 15 July 2016.

26. Mark Urban, "Accelerating extinction risk from climate change," *Science*, Vol. 348, No. 6234, 1 May 2015.

27. John Cook *et al*, "Consensus on consensus: a synthesis of consensus estimates on human-caused global warming," *Environmental Research Letters*, Vol. 11, No. 4, 13 April 2016.

28. John Cook *et al*, "Quantifying the consensus on anthropogenic global warming in the scientific literature," *Environmental Research Letters*, Vol. 8, No. 2, 15 May 2013.

29. Amy Lieberman and Susanne Rust, "Big Oil braced for global warming while it fought regulations," *Los Angeles Times*, 31 December 2015.

30. Ian Talley, "IMF Estimates Trillions in Hidden Fossil-Fuel Costs," *The Wall Street Journal*, 18 May 2015.

31. Justin Farrell, "Corporate funding and ideological polarization about climate change," *Proceedings of the National Academy of Sciences*, Vol. 113, No. 1, 5 January 2016.

32. Peter Hart, "In Denial on Climate Change," *Extra!*, 1 May 2007.

33. Anthony Leiserowitz *et al*, *Climate change in the American mind: April 2014*, New Haven, CT: Yale Project on Climate Change Communication, April 2014.

34. Eduardo Porter, "For Insurers, No Doubts on Climate

Change," *The New York Times*, 14 May 2013.

35. Chris Mooney, "Rex Tillerson's view of climate change: It's just an 'engineering problem,'" *Washington Post*, 14 December 2016.

36. R.K. Pachauri and L.A. Meyer (eds.), *Climate Change 2014 Synthesis Report*, IPCC, Geneva, Switzerland, 2014, p. 60.

37. Camilo Mora *et al*, "Suitable Days for Plant Growth Disappear under Projected Climate Change: Potential Human and Biotic Vulnerability," *PLOS Biology*, 10 June 2015.

38. Benjamin Cook, Toby Ault, and James Smerdon, "Unprecedented 21st century drought risk in the American Southwest and Central Plains," *Science Advances*, Vol. 1, No. 1, 12 February 2015.

39. Jia Liu *et al*, "Particulate air pollution from wildfires in the Western US under climate change," *Climatic Change*, July 2016.

40. Jeremy Pal and Elfatih Eltahir, "Future temperature in southwest Asia projected to exceed a threshold for human adaptability," *Nature Climate Change*, 26 October 2015.

41. Noah Diffenbaugh and Christopher Field, "Changes in Ecologically Critical Terrestrial Climate Conditions," *Science*, Vol. 341, No. 6145, 2 August 2013.

42. John Williams *et al*, "Projected distributions of novel and disappearing climates by 2100 AD," *Proceedings of the National Academy of Sciences*, Vol. 104, No. 14, 30 January 2007.

43. Osvaldo Sala *et al*, "Global Biodiversity Scenarios for the Year 2100," *Science*, Vol. 287, No. 5459, 10 March 2000.

44. Pachauri and Meyer, p. 60.

45. Florent Brient and Tapio Schneider, "Constraints on Climate Sensitivity from Space-Based Measurements of Low-Cloud Reflection," *Journal of Climate*, Vol. 29, No. 16, 28 July 2016.

46. Mathew Hauer *et al*, "Millions projected to be at risk from

sea-level rise in the continental United States," *Nature Climate Change*, Vol. 6, 14 March 2016.

47. Josh Willis and John Church, "Regional Sea-Level Projection," *Science*, Vol. 336, No. 6081, 4 May 2012; Christopher Little *et al*, "Joint projections of US East Coast sea level and storm surge," *Nature Climate Change*, Vol. 5, 21 September 2015.

48. Camilo Mora *et al*, "Biotic and Human Vulnerability to Projected Change in Biogeochemistry over the 21st Century," *PLOS Biology*, Vol. 11, No. 10, October 2013.

49. Ben McNeil and Tristan Sasse, "Future ocean hypercapnia driven by anthropogenic amplification of the natural CO2 cycle," *Nature*, Vol. 529, No. 7586, 20 January 2016.

50. Boris Worm *et al*, "Impacts of Biodiversity Loss on Ocean Ecosystem Services," *Science*, Vol. 314, No. 5800, 3 November 2006.

51. Kolbert, *The Sixth Extinction*, p. 130, 118.

52. Benjamin Strauss *et al*, "Carbon choices determine US cities committed to futures below sea level," *Proceedings of the National Academy of Sciences*, Vol. 112, No. 44, 3 November 2015.

53. Christophe McGlade and Paul Ekins, "The geographical distribution of fossil fuels unused when limiting global warming to 2°C," *Nature*, Vol. 517, 8 January 2015.

54. Trip Gabriel and Coral Davenport, "Calls for Oversight in West Virginia Went Unheeded," *The New York Times*, 13 January 2014; Alexandra Berzon and Kris Maher, "Chemical-Spill Site Avoided Broad Regulatory Scrutiny," *The Wall Street Journal*, 13 January 2014.

55. Frederick Douglass in Philip Foner and Yuval Taylor, ed, *Frederick Douglass: Selected Speeches and Writings*, Chicago, IL: Chicago Review Press, 1999, p. 196.

Chapter 5

Socialism and Freedom
Democratic Economic Organization

Economic equality is not social liberation. It is just this which Marxism and all the other schools of authoritarian Socialism have never understood... The urge for social justice can only develop properly and be effective, when it grows out of man's sense of personal freedom and is based on that. In other words *Socialism will be free, or it will not be at all.*
Rudolf Rocker[1]

The public life of countries with limited freedom is so poverty-stricken, so miserable, so rigid, so unfruitful, precisely because, through the exclusion of democracy, it cuts off the living sources of all spiritual riches and progress... Socialism in life demands a complete spiritual transformation in the masses degraded by centuries of bourgeois class rule.
Rosa Luxemburg[2]

With capitalism revealed as a system of power over society, information, government and the environment, we've got to consider alternatives. This can be a scary prospect for a lot of people, since most of us count on a functioning economic system of some type to stay alive, so tampering with it can make people nervous. But just as societies around the world confronted a system of illegitimate economic power when they outlawed slavery in the nineteenth century, the biggest job for our generation in the twenty-first century is abolishing private ownership of productive capital and the gigantic power arising from it.

It's scary but exciting too, and one good piece of news is

that many of our greatest modern figures have left us a legacy of signposts we can follow on the journey. The main goal will be to see what kinds of social organization could help us limit concentrated power and thus maximize freedom. The main challenge will be to get rid of modern class structures and towering economic power, without in the process creating too strong of another power center, in government or elsewhere. The goal, in other words, is to build a free socialist society.

With capitalism staggering from crisis to crisis, public support for the idea has only built despite reliably hostile media treatment. Rasmussen Reports, a polling agency that actually tends to skew conservative, reported a finding in 2009 that barely more than half (53 percent) of US adults believe capitalism is better than socialism.[3] Twenty percent preferred socialism — impressive considering the total lack of media support — and those under 30 are almost evenly split. A Pew poll found almost a third of Americans have a positive view of socialism, whatever exactly they feel it means.[4] Let's review the basic idea and see the reaction from the figures most eagerly associated with the call to freedom today — the right wing. I'm sure they'll be very mature about it.

The Big Idea

Socialism, like many political and social traditions, is made up of a variety of different schools and therefore different definitions of what the idea is. There tends to be a core of features that a socialist economic system would be expected to have, including equality and a limit to the scale of private property. However, the most essential element of the socialist tradition is workforce control over production and investment — economic democracy.

What would social control over the economy look like? On the individual level, it would mean that when you go to work, you and your coworkers would have access to the information that management usually keeps to itself, and you would together be in charge of work decisions—what to produce, how much and using what methods. In other words, a democratic workplace.

But of course a decent standard of living requires a great deal of coordination with other workplaces, to keep necessary goods and services flowing through their often long production chains in a reasonably efficient fashion. This communication across industries is enormously helped by today's sophisticated telecommunication technology, which could also allow different workforces to collaborate together to satisfy an agreed-upon plan. This interaction among different production units, run by their own workforces, is called "free association," and requires that workers be in charge of the capital equipment and the installations they need to work. It also demands a broad desire to cooperate toward economic goals on a consensual, democratic basis, a priority called "solidarity."

Organization within communities would probably be essential, too—to ensure that production is carried on safely and that local areas will be able to prosper economically. These kinds of coordination will require extensive expertise, as do many areas of the economy. This is fine—socialism isn't opposed to expertise, just the practice of granting *power* to those with that expertise. Doctors and surgeons have enormous technical skill, but that skill doesn't usually give them the authority to make you get an organ transplant without your consent. The same should be true with economic planning and management, since planners and managers are after all skilled workers, and their products—economic plans—should be chosen democratically by representatives of affected workers, neighborhoods and the broader economy.

These basic contours would mean a much freer society than our current capitalist one. Obviously, this bottom-up picture of running an economy is very different from the countries called "socialist" in recent history, a point we'll come back to. But with this basic description in hand of workforce control over investment and the means of production, how have conservatives taken to the idea?

The Right's view since the advent of the movement is that socialism would mean tyranny, while the free market involves no authority or power over anyone. By now we've seen how the latter claim is worthless and sadly the first claim fares no better. The Right's view was given by Friedman, when he made the typical claim that socialism requires total state control over the economy, where "all jobs are under the direct control of political authorities."[5] Hayek, for his part, claimed "socialism means the abolition of private enterprise, of private ownership of the means of production, and the creation of a system of 'planned economy' in which the entrepreneur working for profit is replaced by a central planning body."[6]

A founder of the archconservative "Austrian" economics tradition, Ludwig von Mises, gave another great example of hoary European reactionary thinking in his *The Anti-Capitalistic Mentality*. Like other libertarians, he insisted that "Wealth can be acquired only by serving the customers," and "Here everybody's station in life depends on his own doing."[7] From this he concluded that in a market economy, "It is... exclusively your fault if you do not outstrip" the successful figures in society. And since "merit alone" decides your station, "the unsuccessful feel themselves insulted and humiliated. Hate and enmity against all those who superseded them must result."[8] Mises, then, attributed socialist movements to emotions of jealousy and resentment.

Following their long-running pattern, none of these authors feels the obligation to include more than a breathtakingly few quotes or citations from any actual socialists of any stripe. Most often, no figure on the Left is quoted at all, let alone the strongest advocates. Another expression of their intellectual opportunism, this also helps them completely fail to register the central feature of socialism—worker control.

Hayek argued that freedom should be confined to its negative, not positive, meaning:

> ... freedom from coercion, freedom from the arbitrary power of other men, release from the ties which left the individual no choice but obedience to the orders of a superior to whom he was attached. The new freedom promised, however, was to be freedom from necessity... Freedom in this sense is, of course, merely another name for power or wealth... The demand for the new freedom was thus only another name for the old demand for an equal distribution of wealth.

He added that "the promise of greater freedom has become one of the most effective weapons of socialist propaganda."[9]

Any downward redistribution of wealth has been total anathema for the political Right throughout history, based in traditionally powerful social classes that tend to own a disproportionately large share of the world's money and productive assets. So, while defenders of capitalism openly oppose the positive concept of freedom, they claim negative freedom is provided by the market. But the market in fact fails to uphold the negative "freedom from" coercion, which is opposed to concentrated power, since capitalism is itself a system of power for all the reasons reviewed in Chapter 1. So in reality capitalism fails to meet *either* of these standards of freedom.

But Hayek's basic connection of the socialist ideals of equality and classlessness to positive freedom is essentially correct. That goal was also condemned by the Friedmans, who prefer equality of opportunity to what they call "equality of outcome. Everyone should have the same level of living or of income, should finish the race at the same time. Equality of outcome is in clear conflict with liberty."[10] This is immediately pretty weak—I've never seen a race where the loser is starved to death, but this is very much in the kitty if you lose in the global marketplace. Some Right writers have been slightly more reasonable on this point, as when Hayek conceded sensibly that "What socialism promised was not an absolutely equal, but a more just and more equal, distribution. Not equality in the absolute sense but 'greater equality' is the only goal which is seriously aimed at."[11] And in fact many socialists will countenance somewhat higher incomes for those engaged in very unpleasant or productive work. But the point is adequate equality, such that no one holds major *power* over anyone and no *classes* of people have that ability.

Also, there is the claim that making dramatically more money than others is an indispensible incentive to encourage people to work. Hayek again claims "At least for great numbers some external pressure is needed if they are to give their best."[12] The Friedmans state coldly that the market created "the incentive to transform our society over the past two centuries... Of course, there were many losers along the way—probably more losers than winners. We don't remember their names. But for the most part they went in with their eyes open."[13] Their outcome as beggars and prisoners is an acceptable loss requiring no comment, apparently.

The Right's other common insistence, that socialism means "big government" and "government control over all jobs," struggles with the fact that the core socialist idea, of workforce control over capital and investment, overlaps heavily with the platform of anarchism, the revolutionary cousin of socialism. Daniel Guerin literally wrote the book on *Anarchism*, which in this school means a very organized society, not a chaotic lack of order but lack of power, heavily based on grassroots organization and worker control in the area of the economy. He viewed anarchism as closely related to the more bottom-up schools of socialism, which he called "libertarian socialism," for which "the ideal to be pursued must surely be this direct democracy which, if pressed to the limits in both economic self-management and territorial administration, would destroy the last vestiges of any kind of authority."[14] To Guerin, this was a major plus, as economic and political power are seen to be enemies of freedom, as this book has reviewed. It's hard to square the insistence of every right-wing radio host that socialism means Big Brother's hand on your shoulder, if you consider that one of the wings of socialism is known as anarchism.

This basic picture of socialism as economic democracy, run through some form of worker organization, was at the heart of socialist thinking for many years, reaching its best expression in writers like Anton Pannekoek. A mid-century Dutch scientist and Marxist, his book *Workers' Councils* is almost a manual on healthy socialist organization. A sampling:

> The great task of the workers is the organization of production on a new basis... Collaboration of equal companions replaces the command of masters and obedience of servants... The ruling body in this shop-organization is the entirety of the collaborating workers. They assemble to discuss matters and in assembly take their decisions... In great factories and plants the number of workers is too large to gather in one meeting, and far too large for a real and thorough discussion. Here decisions can only be taken in two steps, by the combined action of assemblies of the separate sections of the plant, and assemblies of central committees of delegates... The delegates constituting them have been sent by sectional assemblies with special instructions; they return to these assemblies to report on the discussion and its result, and after further deliberation the same or other delegates may go up with new instructions... information is not restricted to the personnel of the shop; it is a public matter, open to all outsiders.[15]

Rudolf Rocker, a German social philosopher, agreed, writing thoughtfully that:

... a Socialist economic order cannot be created by the decrees and statutes of a government, but only by the solidaric collaboration of the workers with hand or brain in each special branch of production; that is, through the taking over the management of all plants by the producers themselves... [practical experience] has shown us that economic questions in the Socialist meaning cannot be solved by a government... If the world could be set free by decrees, there would long ago have been no problems left in Russia.[16]

Erich Fromm, the influential social psychologist, supported a not dissimilar "communitarian socialism," in which "every working person would be an active and responsible participant, where work would be attractive and meaningful, where capital would not employ labor, but labor would employ capital."[17] Bertrand Russell, the eminent British philosopher, explored these issues for years, generally maintaining that "the ultimate political power should be democratic... Unless there is popular control, there can be no reason to expect the State to conduct its economic enterprises except for its own enrichment, and therefore exploitation will merely take a new form. Democracy, accordingly, must be accepted as part of the definition of a Socialist regime."[18]

This focus on economic democracy and workforce control does indeed have some obstacles to contend with, like the issue of the industrial scale of operation. Ron Reosti writes in the enjoyable anthology *Imagine: Living in a Socialist USA*, that "despite the destructiveness of corporate power in our current society, some enterprises of that size will continue to exist in a socialist economy. Their economies of scale will be beneficial, provided they are run democratically."[19] Richard Wolff, a prominent Marxist economist, suggests workers "must function collectively as their own board of directors," within democratically organized representative bodies across industries and regions. "Defined in this way, socialism would entail a specific kind of interconnected democratization of the economy and the society."[20]

These different conceptions of social control of investment represent a healthy diversity of emphasis and broad agreement on some of the fundamental principles of a socialist economy. And this participatory strain of socialism is as native to the US as the rest of the world, shown when American labor leader and Socialist Party presidential candidate Eugene Debs denied "that the industries can be taken over and operated by the workers without being industrially organized." This was meant in addition to the broader political action with which Debs is more identified.[21]

A similarly bottom-up approach to socialism was suggested by US economists Michael Albert and Robin Hahnel in their very stimulating but little remembered book *Unorthodox Marxism*, which proposed democratic councils of workplaces as one of "socialism's defining contours." They suggest "Councils are conducive to direct communication, long-term personal relationships, and conflict mediation involving all parties equally," with the socialist goal that "work will take on a new meaning. No longer controlled from without, instead of being a dreaded means to attain the end of leisure time consumption... work will become an *end in itself*... The councils will eventually transform the workplace into an arena where people can effectively engage their creative powers."[22]

As far as more orthodox Marxist approaches, this most prominent school within the broad socialist tradition has a conflicted record on the issues of power and freedom that have dominated this book. Until the 1910s, the heart of the Marxist movement was represented by figures like Pannekoek, or Rosa Luxemburg, who held that socialist movements depend "on the organization and the direct, independent action of the masses."[23] She saw that economic democracy "possesses a powerful corrective—namely, the living movement of the masses, their unending pressure. And the more democratic the institutions, the livelier and stronger the pulse-beat of the political life of the masses, the more direct and complete is their influence."[24]

On the other hand, V.I. Lenin, who became the face of global communism after the Russian Revolution led to the creation of the USSR, has a shifting record on the nature of socialist organization. Before gaining power, his views tended to align with the socialist majority that Pannekoek and Luxemburg represented. Lenin agreed with and indeed emphasized the traditional Marxist concept that the state must "wither away" after power is no longer in the hands of capitalists. In *The State and Revolution* he wrote that socialist parliaments or republics would still be inadequate since "democracy is *also* a state," meaning that even democratic states are power systems, too.[25] In the course of democratizing the economy, he said the state must "transform" from its current authoritarian form "into something which is no longer a state in the proper sense."[26]

Despite these rather anarchist-esque descriptions of worker control, Lenin talked a very different line once in power in traditionally authoritarian Russia, and his actual practice in the Soviet Union will be explored in a moment. He came to reject what he called "Left communism," meaning those socialists who demanded worker control over economic activity, rather than a centralized state allegedly working in their interest. While Luxemburg celebrated the development of the intellect of the people, Lenin held that party elites had a duty of "awakening and enlightening the undeveloped, downtrodden, ignorant peasant *masses*," and party members "must not sink to the level of the masses, to the level of the backward strata of the class."[27] And certainly, Lenin's dictator-like behavior once in power included orders that the Central Committee should dictate to local committees, appoint their leadership and decide the organizational rules.

Many socialists strenuously opposed Lenin's elitist views, including Luxemburg, who claimed that "The ultra-centralism asked by Lenin is full of the sterile spirit of the over-seer. It is not a positive and creative spirit."[28] Mocking his claim that "it is no longer the proletarians, but certain intellectuals in our party who need to be educated in the matters of organization and discipline," she wrote *"Nothing will more surely enslave a young labor movement to an intellectual elite hungry for power than this bureaucratic strait jacket."*[29] To this socialist tradition, Leninism was a right-wing deviation and really a rejection of the socialist ideals of broad participation in social and economic decisions, and the hope that the man and woman in the street can freely share leadership roles without a need for bosses and enforcers.

Built into many of these different descriptions of socialist structures is a need and a desire for a spiritual change among humanity, with the goal of waking up the millions of us who trudge into work every day and are ground down into a passive role where we take orders from the top. Socialism as discussed here would contribute to a spiritual change involving empowerment of the rank-and-file workingman and woman, helping them to feel capable of contributing to not just the muscle but the brains of the economic process. Socialism would both promote and require this change, as the main part of the workforce would be participating in the economic decision-making currently monopolized by the owners and managers of capital. It would require them to strongly desire free and fair outcomes, and prioritize working in solidarity with other democratic workplaces through free association. It would transform humankind.

Importantly, a strong tendency among people discussing or debating changes in social organization is to propose (or demand) a full blueprint of the proposed social structure. This is very understandable, in our scientific and engineered age when diagrammatic representation is naturally prized. However, the diversity of views quoted in this book suggests that our level of understanding of social structures is far more modest than our understanding of engines and computers.

All this means is that the proper approach to these issues is an experimental one—instead of mapping the future society out in detail, we should be encouraging different peoples and communities and industries to try out different methods and configurations of participatory socialism. That can accompany the political effort that tends to dominate headlines. This experimental approach would acknowledge our limited understanding of social evolution, follow the scientific approach we rely on everywhere else, and allow for different peoples and economies to play to their own strengths and explore the various possibilities within a broadly socialist economic system, where important productive property is not owned and controlled by a small upper crust.

A number of radical theoreticians and economists have, however, prepared rather detailed projections for how societies could be organized to allow for the maximum level of democracy and grassroots participation in economic decisions. One of the best-known examples is Parecon, a proposed system of economic organization based on councils and recursive decision-making developed by Albert and Hahnel. Proposals like these are quite handy as jumping-off points for discussion and socialist creative thinking, but we should also have the humility to realize that we're unlikely to get major social change right the first time, and that different peoples and industries will naturally take to different and diverse variants on the core idea.

Having seen how socialist ideas might broaden human freedom, and the Right's somewhat disingenuous response, we should consider an important technique of resisting socialism: repressing its most prominent advocates.

Sanitized Radicals

Years ago the conservative *National Review* happily described the Friedmans' memoir, *Two Lucky People*, including how "Rose Friedman quotes that all-too true adage, which is really the enduring message of this book, that 'If one is not a socialist before the age of thirty, one has no heart; if one remains a socialist after that age of thirty, one has no head."[30] This is a classic saw on the Right.

Someone should tell that to notorious imbecile Albert Einstein, who wrote about the need "to stop the intolerable tyranny of the owners of the means of production (land, machinery) over the wage-earners, in the broadest sense of the term."[31] In 1949 he wrote an extensive essay on his political and economic views for the first issue of the great socialist journal *Monthly Review*:

The economic anarchy of capitalist society as it exists today is, in my opinion, the real source of the evil... Insofar as the labor contract is "free," what the worker receives is determined not by the real value of the goods he produces, but by his minimum needs and by the capitalists' requirements for labor power in relation to the number of workers competing for jobs... Private capital tends to become concentrated in few hands, partly because of competition among the capitalists, and partly because technological development and the increasing division of labor encourage the formation of larger units of production at the expense of smaller ones. The result of these developments is an oligarchy of private capital the enormous power of which cannot be effectively checked even by a democratically organized political society. This is true since the members of legislative bodies are selected by political parties, largely financed or otherwise influenced by private capitalists who, for all practical purposes, separate the electorate from the legislature... Moreover, under existing conditions, private capitalists inevitably control, directly or indirectly, the main sources of information (press, radio, education). It is thus extremely difficult, and indeed in most cases quite impossible, for the individual citizen to come to objective conclusions and to make intelligent use of his political rights... I am convinced there is only *one* way to eliminate these grave evils, namely through the establishment of a socialist economy, accompanied by an educational system which would be oriented toward social goals. In such an economy, the means of production are owned by society itself and are utilized in a planned fashion.[32]

Einstein was explicitly skeptical that the workforce is "free," and indeed recognized the "enormous power" of concentrated capital. Rose Friedman and the *National Review* might have considered Einstein's position before shooting off their mouths about dumb socialists.

Another man "with no head" was civil rights hero Martin Luther King, whose critical view of economic power and support for labor was reviewed in Chapter 1. Although rewritten by mainstream media and scholarship as a liberal mainly focused on segregation and voting rights, he grew significantly more radical over his too-short career. Notably, at the time of his receipt of the Nobel Prize in 1964, he told the press "We feel we have much to learn from Scandinavia's democratic socialist tradition," although the extensive Nordic social support system does not extend to full worker control. More revealingly, while jailed in Selma, Alabama, King's words are recorded as, "If we are going to achieve real equality, the United States will have to adopt a modified form of socialism."[33] Very few Americans are aware of this aspect of King's thought, but it certainly shaped his activism, which grew more radical and fully political until his assassination while supporting a public sanitation workers' strike.

Mahatma Gandhi had over his career conflicted views of the subject, with Norman Finkelstein's *What Gandhi Says* quoting his "hope" that India's independence fight was "only part of the general struggle of colonial peoples against world capitalism and imperialism." On the other hand, he didn't support the key socialist goal of relieving great property owners of their productive property. But he can surely speak with some authority about how powerless people can change society: "[C] apitalists were after all few in number. The workers were many. But capital was well organized and had learnt to combine. If labor realized its inherent strength and the secret of combination it would rule capital instead of being ruled by it."[34]

Or consider George Orwell, who is probably more identified than any other English-speaking writer with indicting the horrors of communist totalitarianism. His books *Animal Farm* and *1984* are globally known for their satires of Stalinist thought control, his writing is cited by the Friedmans and other conservatives, and his work is often found in conservative and even libertarian book catalogs.[35] This is pretty hilarious, considering for example that Orwell wrote in 1946 that "Every line of serious work that I have written since 1936 has been written, directly or indirectly, *against* totalitarianism and *for* democratic socialism, as I understand it."[36]

Elsewhere, when Orwell described his experiences fighting fascism during the Spanish Civil War in his famous *Homage to Catalonia*, he observed that while there was "a section of the Socialists, standing for workers' control," there were other nominal socialists calling for "centralized government and a militarized army."[37] This cleavage in the socialist tradition will come up in the next section, but for Orwell socialism required not only "common ownership of the means of production," but also "approximate equality of incomes (it need be no more than approximate), political democracy, and abolition of all hereditary privilege," aiming for "a world-state of free and equal human beings."[38]

Perhaps with a premonition of Friedman and Hayek themselves, Orwell also remarked that "In every country in the world a huge tribe of party-hacks and sleek little professors are busy 'proving' that Socialism means no more than a planned state-capitalism with the grab-motive left intact. But fortunately there also exists a vision of Socialism quite different from this," describing a "classless society."[39] And in *The Road to Wigan Pier*, Orwell's study of the English working class, he found that capitalism "makes freedom impossible," and that "The only thing *for* which we can combine is the underlying ideal of Socialism: justice and liberty."[40]

A yet more inspirational figure is Malala Yousafzai, the brave Pakistani girl who was shot in the head by Taliban gunmen for her activism for girls' education in Pakistan. Her trip to the US, and meeting with Obama, were heavily covered by US commercial media, celebrating her heroic defiance of fundamentalist terrorism. However, the media studiously kept from mentioning two facts, one of which was her admonishment of the president for his global program of "extrajudicial" drone assassinations, which she said were both morally wrong and only creating more enemies of the country. But also unmentioned was her participation in a Marxist summer school and her message to a Pakistani Marxist convention saying "I am convinced Socialism is the only answer and I urge all comrades to take this struggle to a victorious conclusion. Only this will free us from the chains of bigotry and exploitation."[41] That bit stayed off the front pages.

There are many more examples like this, with global figures from Mandela to Picasso with a history of open, bold socialist views of different types. The immediate lesson is that Rose Friedman and the *National Review* are perhaps mistaken about the mental weakness of anyone holding a socialist worldview, but we could also consider the Western world's educational system's tendency to cleanse all these prominent figures of their dirty socialist radicalism. Meanwhile, the Right can foam at the mouth about the schools being a communist burden, churning out students indoctrinated with left-wing propaganda. Which somehow misses its best opportunities, apparently.

Bolshit

By far the most effective weapon used in the capitalist world to resist the sensible logic and humane appeal of socialism is the alleged socialist structure of Soviet Russia and the rest of the "communist bloc." The USSR, or Union of Soviet Socialist Republics, was held up for generations in the West as an example of what happens with socialism—a hideous, bloody Stalinist dictatorship. Friedman, for example, claimed in *Capitalism and Freedom* that the breakup of the Soviet Union "brought to a dramatic end an experiment of some seventy years between two alternative ways of organizing an economy: top-down versus bottom-up; central planning and control versus private markets; more colloquially, socialism versus capitalism."[42]

The idea that a comparison between the US and the USSR is a fair trial of anything, let alone something approaching a scientific experiment, reveals very clearly the totally politicized sham of a scientist that Friedman and his fellow travelers are. Absolutely no one with an actual sense of scientific conduct would suggest such a thing, because experiments are fundamentally based on similar starting conditions. When testing a new drug, real scientists proceed by trying it out on multiple sets of test rats that have identical diets, exercise, living arrangements and social activity, with the only difference being the presence or absence of the drug. That way, any differences in outcome are clearly due to the drug and not some other factor.

But the US and Russia are hugely dissimilar, even in just their economic conditions. Russia has perennially been a poor, thin-soiled, underdeveloped peasant dictatorship. The US is a young society with hugely productive land and climate, with a tradition of republican government as well as markets. The largest land war in human history occurred when the USSR was invaded by Nazi Germany, right in the middle of this alleged "experiment," with losses north of 20 million people; meanwhile the US was the only major World Ward II belligerent with no combat at all on its own national soil. The fact that economists, and political scientists across the spectrum, are so prepared to put the Cold War episode down as anything like an experiment shows that their "scientific" work is a disgraceful fraud and an opportunistic sham.

A helpful contribution to contrasting the Stalinist empire and the ideals of socialism is Noam Chomsky's essay "The Soviet Union Versus Socialism," which sensibly recognizes that:

> The terminology of political and social discourse is vague and imprecise and constantly debased by the contributions of ideologists of one or another stripe. Still, these terms have at least some residue of meaning... Mastery over production by the producers is the essence of socialism... the essential element of the socialist ideal remains: to convert the means of production into the property of freely associated producers and thus the social property of people who have liberated themselves from exploitation by their master.[43]

On the other hand, "The Leninist antagonism to the most essential features of socialism was evident from the very start," quoting Lenin's observation that "we passed from workers' control to the creation of the Supreme Council of National Economy." Chomsky, somewhat like Rosa Luxemburg above, is skeptical of there having been any socialist structures present at all in post-revolutionary Soviet Russia, and concludes from the record that Lenin and Trotsky "destroyed every vestige of socialism" in Russia.

Certainly, the fact that the USSR and other Leninist countries had a centrally planned economy does not itself make them socialist. Einstein himself observed that "it is necessary to remember that a planned economy is not yet socialism. A planned economy as such may be accompanied by the complete enslavement of the individual."[44] For his own part, Orwell wrote "In my opinion, nothing has contributed so much to the corruption of the original ideal of socialism as the belief that Russia is a socialist country and that every act of its rulers must be excused, if not imitated."[45]

Notably, the "R" in USSR stands for Republic and most of the so-called socialist countries used the term, as do a multitude of oppressive Third World dictatorships. Yet, Friedman and other apologists for capitalism don't try to take the Soviet use of that word to oppose the idea of having a republic and elections. Only the socialist part of this fraud is associated with these dictatorships, in order to defame it. The Western world still needs the pretension of its republic, so that is simply recognized to be a morally respectable idea being cynically used by Russia, China and others to make themselves sound better. More sensibly, we should apply that logic to all the positive ideals they defamed, including socialism.

A similar point applies to the many political parties calling themselves "socialist" in the developed world, which work not for democratic control over production and investment but for mild reforms to today's neoliberal capitalism — social welfare and unemployment insurance, more access to education and healthcare, greater voter participation and such. Often associated with nations of western Central and Northern Europe, this version of parliamentary socialism (or "social democracy") isn't that radical, since it leaves private ownership of large-scale property in place. However, it can still be a very valuable lifeline for struggling people and can push the limits of reform within capitalism. Today, this political strain is quite visible in political figures like Bernie Sanders in the US and Jeremy Corbyn in the UK.

While these are perfectly reasonable short-term reforms that should be supported, they're far from anything like a seriously socialist platform. Chris Maisano observed in the useful book *The ABCs of Socialism*:

> For all of Bernie Sanders's virtues, his campaign for president has only thickened the fog of ideological confusion. At one campaign's stop last year, he endorsed the thinking behind the most of simplistic of... memes: 'When you go to your public library, when you call your fire department or the police department, what do you think you're calling? These are socialist institutions.' By that logic any sort of collective project funded by tax dollars and accomplished through government action is socialism... It's one thing to identify public libraries with socialism. They operate according to democratic principles of access and distribution, providing services to all regardless of one's ability to pay.[46]

But none of this means workforce control over the economy since the social democratic picture of socialism is mainly expanded government services within a market economy. And as Maisano also points out, "because all of those purportedly socialist programs have been won without fundamentally challenging private property," there's no recognition of the power or the owning class or any "need for a decisive confrontation with the owners of capital and their political allies."[47]

Many of today's social democrat parties are affiliates of the Socialist International, which as Gerard Di Trolio wrote in *Jacobin* magazine is "Socialist in Name Only."[48] This can be seen quite quickly by reviewing its membership list, which includes the austerity-mongering George Papandreou, the former Greek prime minister, about as far as you can get from a socialist program. Egypt's National Democratic Party, the ruling apparatus of deposed dictator Hosni Mubarak, was in good standing for many years, along with the UK Labour Party and US Democratic Party, which in recent decades are full-on appendages of neoliberalism (see Chapter 3). And indeed, during the era of independence movements for Europe's former colonies, "the SI was encouraging the formation of center-left parties in the newly democratizing countries as a means of marginalizing more radical forces."

For many years, socialists haven't been naïve about the Soviet dictatorship, or the sometimes aggressive but commonly weak-sauce semi-reforms of the UK Labour Party, or any of the allegedly "socialist" Third World states. The fact that these drab dictatorships tried to tramp themselves up with words borrowed from humanity's highest aspirations, like "republic," "socialist" and "democracy," doesn't tarnish those valuable ideals as much as the reputations of shallow intellectuals, on all sides, who take them seriously.

Crashes to Ashes, Bust to Rust

The world of the early twenty-first century is staggering under neoliberal capitalism and the confused popular responses to it, like Brexit and the Trump administration, but opportunities for freedom have not disappeared. With people's faith in the system of market power fading, as suggested by today's electoral upsets and the worldwide polling mentioned earlier, it's a great time to take stock of world currents, and evaluate where organizational and educational efforts can have an effect.

Today's social struggles are very much a race against time ecologically. Millennia of human exploitation of natural systems have had a cumulative effect, especially since the advent of industrial capitalism and its centuries of exponential cost externalizing. The effects are growing increasingly ominous and indeed scientists are finding that the rate of change is picking up, as reviewed in Chapter 4. Notably, large craters have begun appearing mysteriously in the great permafrost expanses of Russian Siberia.[49] While investigations continue, geoscientists suggest that warming soils are releasing methane hydrates, which as the ground warms can transition to gaseous methane that bursts out of the ground in giant ejections. Notably, methane is itself a more potent greenhouse gas than carbon dioxide. The air near their lower reaches has a methane concentration of 9.6 percent, far higher than the normal concentration of 0.000179 percent.[50] A smoking gun, indeed a smoking 90-foot crater.

Meanwhile, in the US state of Florida, made up of low-lying, porous limestone that is particularly vulnerable to climate change and rising sea levels, it's reported that the very mention of these subjects has been prevented by the political authorities. Despite administration denials, the *Miami Herald* claims that the state's Department of Environmental Protection officials "have been ordered not to use the term 'climate change' or 'global warming' in any official communications, emails, or reports," under the administration of Republican Governor Rick Scott.[51] The unwritten policy can be seen in state reports, which no longer mention climate change except when directly referencing the titles of previous reports from before the pitiful gag rule was imposed. A former staff member says "Sea-level rise was to be referred to as 'nuisance flooding.'"

A summary of the possible future is given in the updated edition of *Limits to Growth*, a classic book analyzing how far the limits of the Earth's natural systems can be pushed, in various different scenarios. Across most of them, the study team concludes "the world system does not totally run out of land or food or resources or pollution absorption capability. What it runs out of is *the ability to cope*."[52] This indeed has been the character of the final stages of many previous societies, unable to handle the endless seemingly different problems arising from their overexploitation of the natural systems they depended on. It's a sacred necessity that socialism not inherit a cursed Earth.

Politically, the current period is notoriously volatile, with US global hegemony partially waning but remaining violent, and entering a new, unstable period accompanied by increasingly dramatic acts of state and jihadi terrorism. Deranged right-wing media, both corporate and Islamist, drive people with underdeveloped critical thinking skills to violence on a regular, escalating basis. The environmental crisis also feeds into this, with scientists proposing that the disruptions of climate heating, droughts and flooding are aggravating conflicts. The subject remains controversial among scientists, but most recently a group of researchers has observed that the Syrian Civil War, one of the worst conflicts of our time, was precipitated by a protest movement that partially emerged among desperate and displaced farmers dealing with the worst drought in the history of modern Syria.[53] In this way, climate change is literally turning up the heat on global conflicts.

For these and other reasons, the Bulletin of the Atomic Scientists moved its "Doomsday Clock," which represents the risk to humanity of a terminal nuclear conflict, to only three minutes to midnight, the most dangerous reading since the renewal of the Cold War in 1984.[54] The global refusal to deal with climate change was part of this calculation, raising the odds that someday humanity will wake up to the day of a thousand suns.

Today's world situation sees the large majority of the human race living in the Third World, or what today is called the "Global South," as opposed to the Northern nations that developed economically—Europe, the US, Canada, and Japan. Citizens of the developed North (or the "West") tend to be almost totally ignorant of conditions in the South, as well as the North's history of keeping them there, part of which came up in Chapter 3. Maybe the most important issue to consider here is development—the process of income growth and diversification that takes countries out of Third World conditions. Since this process is the greatest hope of the large majority of people in the world, it's crucial to recognize the role that the developed Northern countries, in the form of the G7, played in the 1970s in blocking the New International Economic Order (NIEO) promoted by the global South, in the form of the G77 and the broader Non-Aligned Movement (NAM).

The NIEO would have obliged the developed North not to merely give a trickle of "development aid" to the desperately poor South, but rather capital grants for economic development, higher and more stable prices for the raw materials that many of the poor economies rely on after the colonial redesigns of their economies, and transfer of sophisticated technologies to the poor countries. After all, the Northern countries themselves developed behind big tariff barriers and free foreign technology. However, the G7 was generally opposed to this prioritization of development of the poorest, with the US taking a leadership role in defeating it, a phenomenal story recounted in Vijay Prashad's overpowering book *The Poorer Nations*.

Instead, the North successfully implemented the current neoliberal standards—treaties promoting free trade, private corporate investment in the poorer economies and an unforgiving stance toward Third World debt. The former colonial powers were able to "break up the unholy alliance" among the NAM, but among the G7 "Solidarity in bargaining must be achieved," as it was explained by the then Chancellor of West Germany, Helmut Schmidt.[55] And despite literally five centuries of the global South being colonies and captive markets of the developed world, US President Reagan mocked the Third World's proposals for their development: "Others mistake compassion for development, and claim massive transfers of wealth somehow, miraculously, will produce new well-being."[56] A truly heinous historical remark, in light of the record.

The effects of these developments cast a long shadow— including on demographic development. As the developed Northern countries dictated to the South through the long colonial era and the "neoliberal" period since then, the South's restrained development has kept birth rates high, in the traditional pattern of large families insuring poor parents against old age, even as death rates have fallen with the partial introduction of public health measures, mainly inoculation. *The New York Times* observes that Nigeria, for example, will have the current population of the US in a country the size of Arizona, Nevada and New Mexico in around twenty-five years. Most of the projected increase from today's world population of 7 billion people is expected to occur in sub-Saharan Africa, since "In Asian countries, women's contraceptive use skyrocketed from less than 20 percent to 60 to 80 percent in decades. In Latin America, requiring girls to finish high school correlated with a sharp drop in birth rates."[57] For Africa, however, at least for the moment, "Of the roughly 20 countries where women average more than five children, almost all are in the region."

And with a majority of the world's population now urban, not rural, historian Mike Davis has written the definitive account of the growth of the Third World megacity in his book *Planet of Slums*. The gigantic growth in urban living in the developing world doesn't owe to the traditional city-building dynamics of the Industrial Revolution, which the North experienced: "Since the mid-1980s, the great industrial cities of the South— Bombay, Johannesburg, Buenos Aires, Belo Horizonte, and Sao Paulo—have all suffered massive plant closures and tendential deindustrialization. Elsewhere, urbanization has been more radically decoupled from industrialization, even development *per se*."[58] Indeed, today's cities of the Global South have more to do with the crisis of global agriculture than industrialization and rising living standards.

The worst part of breakneck urbanization, here or in Victorian

England, is as Davis puts it, "Living in Shit."

> Today's poor megacities—Nairobi, Lagos, Bombay, Dhaka, and so on—are stinking mountains of shit that would appall even the most hardened Victorians... Constant intimacy with other people's waste, moreover, is one of the most profound of social divides. Like the universal prevalence of parasites in the bodies of the poor, living in shit, as the Victorians knew, truly demarcates two existential humanities. The global sanitation crisis defies hyperbole. Its origins, as with many Third World urban problems, are rooted in colonialism. The European empires mostly refused to provide modern sanitation and water infrastructures in native neighborhoods... postcolonial regimes from Accra to Hanoi thus inherited huge sanitation deficits that few regimes have been prepared to aggressively remedy.[59]

In Bangalore, the center of India's much-celebrated hi-tech economy, *The Times* observes that "the dark side of the country's rapid economic growth" is its incredible amount of civil garbage. "India's plague," they call it, not counting the actual plague, apparently.[60] While the "garbage crisis grew directly out of its stunning success," a strike by sanitation workers who'd gone unpaid for weeks and "the city running out of abandoned quarries to quietly deliver a day's load" has brought the system to its knees. Now, the city is embracing the "informal system of 15,000 waste workers," peasants who pick through the flood of trash for food or sellable items. These 15,000 garbage pickers are apparently not themselves a demerit to the city's "stunning success."

The growth of mega-slums is occurring even as financial giants and rich governments are buying up Global South real estate at an impressive pace, in a twenty-first century "land rush." *The Guardian* relates that "Leading the rush are international agribusinesses, investment banks, hedge funds, commodity traders, sovereign wealth funds as well as UK pension funds, foundations and individuals attracted by some of the world's cheapest land… Saudi Arabia, along with other Middle Eastern emirate states such as Qatar, Kuwait and Abu Dhabi, is thought to be the biggest buyer."[61] While the lives of people in the South aren't worth much, their land may be, leaving them to scrape by in pestilential urban hells making a living however they can, if they can.

Such industry as is present is conducted on dramatically one-sided class lines. The organization and mobility of capital discussed in Chapter 1 has striking effects in, for example, Bangladesh, the largest producer of textiles after China itself. The headline-making collapse of a garment factory in 2013 at the Rana Plaza complex outside Dhaka killed 1129 and left another 2515 injured, maimed and disabled. The factory had passed safety inspections by a European trade organization, suggesting its audits were a PR fig leaf.

The workforce had evacuated the building the day before the disaster, after a large crack appeared on the building exterior. The workforce isn't stupid. However, the factory management ordered the workers back the next day and "Some workers were threatened with docked pay if they didn't comply. Soon after, the building collapsed," as *The Wall Street Journal* reports.[62] After hundreds of thousands of workers went on strike in protest of the lack of real safety standards, the Bangladeshi government made it somewhat easier for workers to unionize.[63]

This is an impressive activist victory, since in Bangladesh "factory owners, many of whom are also local politicians or members of Parliament, maintain political clout." In fact, over 10 percent of the total seats in the Parliament are held by owners of garment contractors. Yet, a director at Human Rights Watch observes "Had one or more of the Rana Plaza factories been unionized, its workers would have been in a position to refuse to enter the building on Wednesday morning, and thus save their lives."[64] And their limbs, which numerous survivors lost. Once again, worker organization remains a way to pry some power and a bit of freedom from the machinery of capital.

But, unsurprisingly, unions have struggled to survive in Bangladesh against the organized power of the owners of capital, in a continuation of the tradition of violence against worker organization. Closed-circuit cameras outside plants record union activists being beaten by thugs directed by factory management, in one instance with a major US apparel company itself finding that "factory managers directed those attacks," for example one where "a female union president was beaten in the head with an iron rod."[65] Management claimed the violence originated in a worker dispute, but the union simply refers to the videos, showing that "some managers and anti-union workers had arrived early and were strategically placed when buses stopped outside the factory."

Notably, the factory "produced clothes for several international retailers." Milton Friedman often used the easy example of neckties and other garments to illustrate the diverse nature of markets, passing over the more embarrassing cases like utility and transport monopolies. But even here, in an apparently more diverse market, the chic designers use the same dank, deafening, densely packed sweatshops to produce their pretty flash merchandise, provided the roof doesn't fall in.

History suggests that industry has simply outsourced its most dangerous and exploitative work. A century earlier, these heinous industrial accidents occurred in the US instead. As the great radical historian Howard Zinn recounts:

On the afternoon of March 25, 1911, a fire at the Triangle Shirtwaist Company that began in a rag bin swept through the eighth, ninth, and tenth floors, too high for fire ladders to reach. The fire chief of New York had said that his ladders could reach only to the seventh floor... The law said the doors could not be locked during working hours, but at the Triangle Company doors were usually locked so the company could keep track of the employees. And so, trapped, the young women were burned to death at their worktables, or jammed against the locked exit door, or leaped to their deaths down the elevator shafts... When it was over, 146 Triangle workers, mostly women, were burned or crushed to death.[66]

So in some industrial accidents, the workers leap from the building. In others, the building falls down on the workforce. This freedom of choice was totally missed by the Friedmans.

But these tragedies could be almost completely avoided, of course, if human beings no longer worked on a large scale producing goods and services. The long-term process of automation—replacing some kinds of human work with more sophisticated capital equipment—is maybe the clearest instantiation of the irrationality of capitalism. In a socialist world, freeing the workforce from this often dull, repetitive work would be a blessing, but in the market economy it is damnation. For it often puts large parts of the existing workforce out on the streets, with no guarantee that new work will be available to replace it, or that the existing workforce will have any realistic hope of retraining and educating for such new jobs as arise. *The Wall Street Journal* alarmingly reported recently that:

In the Australian outback, for example, mining giant Rio Tinto uses self-driving trucks and drills that need no human operators at iron ore mines. Automated trains will soon carry the ore to a port 300 miles away. The Port of Los Angeles is installing equipment that could cut in half the number of longshoremen needed in a workplace already highly automated. Computers do legal research, write stock reports and news stories, as well as translate conversations; at car dealers, they generate online advertising; and, at banks, they churn out government-required documents to flag potential money laundering—all jobs done by human workers a short time ago.[67]

The conservative paper quotes research agency and academic forecasts projecting that a third of all current jobs will likely be automated within ten years, and half of all jobs in two decades. Anything remotely like these figures is a gigantic change for the human condition and likely not for the better. While the automation of so much arduous human labor might create the millennium under a sensible economic system, under capitalism it means layoffs, disappointment, and huge involuntary life changes and movements of people around the world. Irony loves company!

Importantly in this connection, economist Richard Wolff observes that "had workers been their own directors in the 1970s, they would not have stopped raising workers' real wages while their productivity kept rising," which of course is what happened under neoliberal capitalism.[68] Today's sophisticated information systems could hugely help with the problem of coordinating a democratically run economy, but as long as it remains private, capital will be used more along the lines of today's social media. Facebook and Twitter are thought to be free to use, with many users not realizing that *they* are the product—enormous social media account rolls are presented by these platforms to advertisers willing to pay for the fractured attention span of the users. As we convert our personalities and identities into cleaned-up online avatars of ourselves, we're also bringing up a new generation in a shallow version of social connection, and forcing ourselves into smaller and smaller venues for speech, making it harder to make nuanced points.

With this endless parade of bummer news developments, it's easy to feel down. But being truly pessimistic is pretty cocky, since all we experience today is surprise. The Arab Spring, the Occupy movement, 9/11, the rise of ISIS, the Chicago Republic Windows sit-down strike, the startling success of the Sanders and Trump campaigns, all took us by surprise. Being sure of bad outcomes implies you're somehow not here getting startled with the rest of us.

As Harriet Fraad and Tess Fraad-Wolff write, "Imagine not fearing layoffs! Democracy at work would prevent the terror of job insecurity that plagues Americans. Worker-run companies do not outsource their own jobs."[69] Former slave Frederick Douglass, who stated his opposition to the "wage slavery" that was only a slight improvement over the "chattel slavery" he had been forced into, famously wrote:

> The whole history of the progress of human liberty shows that all concessions yet made to her august claims, have been born of earnest struggle... If there is no struggle there is no progress. Those who profess to favor freedom and yet deprecate agitation, are men who want crops without plowing up the ground, they want rain without thunder and lightning. They want the ocean without the roar of its many waters... Power concedes nothing without a demand. It never did and it never will. Find out just what any people will quietly submit to and you have found out the exact measure of injustice and wrong which will be imposed upon them... The limits of tyrants are prescribed by the endurance of those whom they oppress.[70]

The point is, global conditions will probably continue their current horrifying decline, unless far more men and women start to put some of their time and energy into social and economic activism. Rather than fighting for a "libertarian" world, with more freedom for families of towering fortunes to dominate the world, regular people could work on forming an environmental activist team, or a reading and discussion group, or a labor union. That's a seed to plant in the hope of growing another world, a world that could one day be free of the reign of gold.

A world of free, democratic socialism, answering the prayers of millions of people around the world, would be a very positive legacy to leave. We could have a truly free economy. It could spiritually transform us. A world where the sun shines on a free race of people is worth a little of your free time, so please join your fellow men and women in turning the page of history. Let's steal from the rich and drink to the poor.

Endnotes

1. Rudolf Rocker, *Anarcho-Syndicalism*, London: Pluto Press, 1989, p. 27–8.
2. Rosa Luxemburg, *The Russian Revolution and Leninism or Marxism?* Ann Arbor, MI: Ann Arbor Paperbacks, 1961, p. 70–1.
3. Rasmussen Reports, "Just 53% Say Capitalism Better Than Socialism," 9 April 2009.
4. PewResearch, "Little Change in Public's Response to 'Capitalism,' 'Socialism,'" 28 December 2011.
5. Milton Friedman, *Capitalism and Freedom*, Chicago, IL: University of Chicago Press, 2002, p. 16.
6. Friedrich Hayek, *The Road to Serfdom*, Chicago: University of Chicago Press, 2007, p. 83.
7. Ludwig von Mises, *The Anti-Capitalistic Mentality*, Princeton, NJ: Libertarian Press, 1981, p. 2, 11.
8. *Ibid*, p. 10, 13–14.
9. Hayek, *The Road to Serfdom*, p. 77–8.
10. Milton and Rose Friedman, *Free to Choose*, New York: Harcourt, 1990, p. 128.
11. Hayek, *The Road to Serfdom*, p. 140.
12. *Ibid*, p. 151.

13. Friedmans, *Free to Choose*, p. 138.
14. Daniel Guerin, *Anarchism*, New York: Monthly Review Press, 1960, p. 60.
15. Anton Pannekoek, *Workers' Councils*, Oakland, CA: AK Press, 2003, p. 19–23.
16. Rocker, *Anarcho-Syndicalism*, p. 94–5.
17. Erich Fromm, *The Sane Society*, New York: Fawcett Premier, 1965. P. 248.
18. Bertrand Russell, *In Praise of Idleness and Other Essays*, New York: Routledge, 2004.
19. Ron Reosti, "A Democratically Run Economy Can Replace the Oligarchy," in Francis Golden, *et al*, Eds., *Imagine: Living in a Socialist USA*, New York: HarperCollins, 2014, p. 36.
20. Richard Wolff, *Capitalism Hits the Fan*, Northampton, MA: Olive Branch Press, 2013, p. 212.
21. Debs, *Eugene V. Debs Speaks*, p. 206.
22. Michael Albert and Robin Hahnel, *Unorthodox Marxism*, Boston: South End Press, 1978, p. 258–60.
23. Rosa Luxemburg, *The Russian Revolution and Leninism or Marxism?* p. 86.
24. *Ibid*, p. 62.
25. V.I. Lenin, *The State and Revolution*, London: Penguin Books, 1992, p. 18.
26. *Ibid*, p. 38.
27. V.I. Lenin, *"Left-Wing" Communism, an Infantile Disorder*, New York: International Publishers, 2009, p. 42.
28. Rosa Luxemburg, *The Russian Revolution and Leninism or Marxism?* p. 94.
29. *Ibid*, p. 89–90; p. 102.
30. Stephen Moore, "All Friedmanites Now," *National Review*, Vol. 50, No. 14, 3 August 1998.
31. Albert Einstein, *The World As I See It*, New York: Citadel Press, 1997, p. 74.
32. Albert Einstein, "Why Socialism?" *Monthly Review*, May

33. Douglas Sturm, "Martin Luther King, Jr., as Democratic Socialist," *The Journal of Religious Ethics*, Vol. 18, No. 2, 1990, p. 99.

34. Norman Finkelstein, *What Gandhi Says*, New York: OR Books, 2012, p. 62, 65.

35. Friedmans, *Free to Choose*, p. 135.

36. George Orwell, "Why I Write," *A Collection of Essays*, Orlando, FL: Harcourt Brace & Co, 1981, p. 314.

37. George Orwell, *Homage to Catalonia*, New York: Houghton Mifflin Harcourt, 1980, p. 62.

38. George Orwell, *The Lion and the Unicorn*, Harmondsworth, UK: Penguin, 1986, p. 75–6.

39. Orwell, *Homage to Catalonia*, p. 104.

40. George Orwell, *The Road to Wigan Pier*, Orlando, FL: Harcourt, 1958, p. 179, 216.

41. Convention report, In Defence of Marxism, http://www.marxist.com/historic-32nd-congress-of-pakistani-imt-1.htm.

42. Friedman, *Capitalism and Freedom*, p. viii.

43. Noam Chomsky, "The Soviet Union Versus Socialism," *Our Generation*, Spring/Summer 1986.

44. Albert Einstein, "Why Socialism?" *Monthly Review*, May 1949.

45. George Orwell, "The Freedom of the Press," *The Times Literary Supplement*, 15 September 1972.

46. Chirs Maisano in Bhaskar Sunkara, ed, *The ABCs of Socialism*, London: Verso, 2016, p. 14–15.

47. *Ibid*, p. 15.

48. Gerard Di Trolio, "Socialist in Name Only," *Jacobin*, 28 December 2014.

49. Steven Smith *et al*, "Near-term acceleration in the rate of temperature change," *Nature Climate Change*, 9 March 2015.

50. Katia Msokvitch, "Mysterious Siberian crater attributed to methane," *Nature* News, 31 July 2014.

51. Tristam Korten, "In Florida, officials ban term 'climate change,'" *Miami Herald*, 8 March 2015.
52. Donella Meadows *et al*, *Limits to Growth*, White River Junction, VT: Chelsea Green Publishing, 2004, p. 223.
53. Henry Fountain, "Researchers Link Syrian Conflict to a Drought Made Worse by Climate Change," *The New York Times*, 2 March 2015.
54. The Bulletin of the Atomic Scientists, http://thebulletin.org/timeline.
55. Vijay Prashad, *The Poorer Nations*, London: Verso, 2012, p. 43, 47.
56. *Ibid*, p. 79.
57. Elisabeth Rosenthal, "Nigeria Tested by Rapid Rise in Population," *The New York Times*, 14 April 2012.
58. Mike Davis, *World of Slums*, London: Verso, 2006, p. 13.
59. *Ibid*, p. 138–9.
60. Gardiner Harris, "India's Plague, Trash, Drowns Its Garden City During Strike," *The New York Times*, 26 October 2012.
61. John Vidal, "How food and water are driving a 21st-century African land grab," *The Guardian*, 6 March 2010.
62. Syed Al-Mahmood and Tom Wright, "Collapsed Factory Was Built Without Permit," *The Wall Street Journal*, 25 April 2013.
63. Syed Al-Mahmood, "A Year Later, Rana Plaza Survivors Struggle," *The Wall Street Journal*, 23 April 2014.
64. Syed Al-Mahmood and Tom Wright, "Collapsed Factory Was Built Without Permit," *The Wall Street Journal*, 25 April 2013.
65. Steven Greenhouse, "Union Leaders Attacked at Bangladesh Garment Factories, Investigations Show," *New York Times*, 22 December 2014.
66. Howard Zinn, *A People's History of the United States*, New York: HarperCollins, 1999, p. 326–7.
67. Timothy Aeppel, "What Clever Robots Mean for Jobs," *The*

Wall Street Journal, 24 February 2015.

68. Wolff, *Capitalism Hits the Fan*, p. 214.
69. Harriet Fraad and Tess Fraad-Wolff, "Personal, Emotional, and Sexual Life Without Capitalism," in Francis Golden, *et al*, Eds., *Imagine: Living in a Socialist USA*, p. 78.
70. Frederick Douglass, *Selected Speeches and Writings*, Chicago, IL: Lawrence Hill Books, 1999, p. 367.

Zero Books

CULTURE, SOCIETY & POLITICS

Contemporary culture has eliminated the concept and public figure of the intellectual. A cretinous anti-intellectualism presides, cheer-led by hacks in the pay of multinational corporations who reassure their bored readers that there is no need to rouse themselves from their stupor. Zer0 Books knows that another kind of discourse – intellectual without being academic, popular without being populist – is not only possible: it is already flourishing. Zer0 is convinced that in the unthinking, blandly consensual culture in which we live, critical and engaged theoretical reflection is more important than ever before.

If you have enjoyed this book, why not tell other readers by posting a review on your preferred book site.

Recent bestsellers from Zero Books are:

In the Dust of This Planet
Horror of Philosophy vol. 1
Eugene Thacker
In the first of a series of three books on the Horror of
Philosophy, *In the Dust of This Planet* offers the genre of horror
as a way of thinking about the unthinkable.
Paperback: 978-1-84694-676-9 ebook: 978-1-78099-010-1

Capitalist Realism
Is there no alternative?
Mark Fisher
An analysis of the ways in which capitalism has presented itself
as the only realistic political-economic system.
Paperback: 978-1-84694-317-1 ebook: 978-1-78099-734-6

Rebel Rebel
Chris O'Leary
David Bowie: every single song. Everything you want to know,
everything you didn't know.
Paperback: 978-1-78099-244-0 ebook: 978-1-78099-713-1

Cartographies of the Absolute
Alberto Toscano, Jeff Kinkle
An aesthetics of the economy for the twenty-first century.
Paperback: 978-1-78099-275-4 ebook: 978-1-78279-973-3

Malign Velocities
Accelerationism and Capitalism
Benjamin Noys
Long listed for the Bread and Roses Prize 2015, *Malign Velocities* argues against the need for speed, tracking acceleration as the symptom of the ongoing crises of capitalism.
Paperback: 978-1-78279-300-7 ebook: 978-1-78279-299-4

Meat Market
Female flesh under Capitalism
Laurie Penny
A feminist dissection of women's bodies as the fleshy fulcrum of capitalist cannibalism, whereby women are both consumers and consumed.
Paperback: 978-1-84694-521-2 ebook: 978-1-84694-782-7

Poor but Sexy
Culture Clashes in Europe East and West
Agata Pyzik
How the East stayed East and the West stayed West.
Paperback: 978-1-78099-394-2 ebook: 978-1-78099-395-9

Romeo and Juliet in Palestine
Teaching Under Occupation
Tom Sperlinger
Life in the West Bank, the nature of pedagogy and the role of a university under occupation.
Paperback: 978-1-78279-637-4 ebook: 978-1-78279-636-7

Sweetening the Pill
or How we Got Hooked on Hormonal Birth Control
Holly Grigg-Spall
Has contraception liberated or oppressed women? *Sweetening the Pill* breaks the silence on the dark side of hormonal contraception.
Paperback: 978-1-78099-607-3 ebook: 978-1-78099-608-0

Why Are We The Good Guys?
Reclaiming your Mind from the Delusions of Propaganda
David Cromwell
A provocative challenge to the standard ideology that Western power is a benevolent force in the world.
Paperback: 978-1-78099-365-2 ebook: 978-1-78099-366-9

Readers of ebooks can buy or view any of these bestsellers by clicking on the live link in the title. Most titles are published in paperback and as an ebook. Paperbacks are available in traditional bookshops. Both print and ebook formats are available online.

Find more titles and sign up to our readers' newsletter at http://www.johnhuntpublishing.com/culture-and-politics

Follow us on Facebook
at https://www.facebook.com/ZeroBooks

and Twitter at https://twitter.com/Zer0Books